Tax Guide 202

PROFITS, TAXES, & LLCs

by

Holmes F. Crouch
Tax Specialist

Published by

Allyear Tax Guides

20484 Glen Brae Drive
Saratoga, CA 95070

ISBN 0-944817-65-3

LCCN 2002102085

Printed in U.S.A.

Second Printing

Series 200
Investors & Businesses

Tax Guide 202

PROFITS, TAXES, & LLCs

For other titles in print, see page 224.

The author: **Holmes F. Crouch**

For more about the author, see page 221.

PREFACE

If you are a knowledge-seeking **taxpayer** looking for information, this book can be helpful to you. It is designed to be read — from cover to cover — in about eight hours. Or, it can be "skim-read" in about 30 minutes.

Either way, you are treated to **tax knowledge** . . . *beyond the ordinary.* The "beyond" is that which cannot be found in IRS publications, FedWorld on-line services, tax software programs, Internet chatrooms, or e-mail bulletins.

Taxpayers have different levels of interest in a selected subject. For this reason, this book starts with introductory fundamentals and progresses onward. You can verify the progression by chapter and section in the table of contents. In the text, "applicable law" is quoted in pertinent part. Key phrases and key tax forms are emphasized. Real-life examples are given . . . in down-to-earth style.

This book has 12 chapters. This number provides depth without cross-subject rambling. Each chapter starts with a head summary of meaningful information.

To aid in your skim-reading, informative diagrams and tables are placed strategically throughout the text. By leafing through page by page, reading the summaries and section headings, and glancing at the diagrams and tables, you can get a good handle on the matters covered.

Effort has been made to update and incorporate all of the latest tax law changes that are *significant* to the title subject. However, "beyond the ordinary" does not encompass every conceivable variant of fact and law that might give rise to protracted dispute and litigation. Consequently, if a particular statement or paragraph is crucial to your own specific case, you are urged to seek professional counseling. Otherwise, the information presented is general and is designed for a broad range of reader interests.

The Author

INTRODUCTION

The fear in the heart of every owner of a closely-held business is the potential of a lawsuit. In such a litigious society as the United States, it is not a question of "if" a lawsuit will occur. It is only a matter of time "when" it will occur. When it does, it will be based on some perceived wrongdoing by the business entity itself, or on some alleged misconduct by an owner, manager, employee, or agent thereof. Regardless of what the business activity may be, there is always **that threat** out there.

The target for attack is not so much the assets of the business itself. Most small and closely-held businesses barely keep enough capital on hand to meet their operating needs. Because so, the primary target for lawsuit is the personal assets of the principals of the business: their homes, bank accounts, investments, realty holdings, and future earnings. These targets are all fair game under the "alter ego" theory for piercing the entity shield.

There is an inherent injustice in piercing the entity shield of a small business with extraneous lawsuits having no direct connection to the conduct or misconduct of its owners and managers. For well over 20 years, various state legislatures have wrestled with this problem. To one degree or another, remedial effort was directed at *limiting* the personal liability of unincorporated entrepreneurs, without giving them a green light to violate ordinary business and contract law. Finally, in early 1997, all 50 states (plus the District of Columbia) have agreed upon a new entity form: the LIMITED LIABILITY COMPANY (**LLC**).

So new is the operational concept of an LLC that the Internal Revenue Code does not use the term in any of its business-related sections and subsections. Instead, it is embodied in the term "eligible entity" in Regulation § 301.7701-3: *Classification of certain business entities*. Its two opening sentences read—

> *A business entity that is not classified as a corporation . . . (an eligible entity) can elect its classification for federal tax purposes. An eligible entity with at least two members can elect to be classified as . . .* [an LLC] *partnership.*

The point that we are trying to get across is that it took some 20 years to crystallize the legality of an LLC under consensus state law. We think it will take another 20 years or so before all the tax and legal ramifications are worked out, and before specific sections and subsections of the federal tax code are enacted.

In the meantime, we have this book: *Profits, Taxes, & LLCs.* Our objective is to sidestep the promotional hype and excitement associated with LLCs, and take a closer look at the serious side of this "new darling" of unincorporated business. We are trying to look ahead to see how the LLC concept will fit into the Internal Revenue Code. First and foremost, an LLC is a profit-seeking business. When profits are made, there are taxes to pay. But the manner of doing so involves some unique characteristics of an LLC's own. This is because an LLC is a hybrid entity with the managerial flexibility of a proprietorship, the profit and loss pass-through benefits of a partnership, and the limited personal liability trump card of a corporation. Unlike a corporation, though, an LLC does not enjoy indefinite life.

The feature of "limited liability" does not bestow upon an LLC a free-wheeling, responsibility-avoiding arrangement for exploitative entrepreneurship. Yes, there is intrigue and excitement in those two letters "LL". But they do not extend a right of passage into lots of money without incurring personal obligation in some manner.

The painful reality is that there are articles of organization to be filed with state authorities and fees to be paid; there are operating agreements to be worked out; there is a minimum capital base to be maintained; there are at-risk and not-for-profit rules to be heeded; there are books and records to be kept; there are balance sheets to be balanced; there are tax returns to be filed; and there are contracts with customers, creditors, and suppliers to be honored. In the end, every LLC has to take its place in line demonstrating responsible behavior, as do other entities, both corporate and noncorporate.

CONTENTS

Chapter	Page

Chapter	Page

1

LLC: A HYBRID ENTITY

An LLC Is Not A Corporation, Nor Is It A Trust. It Is More Like A Partnership Where Each Member Has Management Rights, As Though He Were A Sole Proprietor. As Such, An LLC Member Is Both A General Partner And A Limited Partner At The Same Time. Statutorily, There Is No Limit To The Number And Type Of Members Permitted. At Some Number, Though, Management Prudence And Reality Cut In. As With Any Traditional Form Of Small Business, An LLC Must Actively Seek A Profit On A Continuing Basis. Any Net Earnings And Losses Are "Passed Through" To Individual Members Who Are Then Taxed By State And Federal Authorities.

In our Introduction, we tipped you off that an LLC (Limited Liability Company) had some of the operating characteristics of a proprietorship, a partnership, and a corporation. We refer to these three entity types as the "traditional forms" for making money and distributing the net earnings. As such, an LLC can be thought of as a *fourth* entity form for conducting business.

An LLC can conduct any kind of business which is not illegal, and which is not precluded by other legislative acts. The term "other legislative acts" pertains to those special laws (state and federal) that are directed at banking, insurance, financial services, public utilities, churches, charities, exempt organization (pension plans, hospitals, labor unions), private foundations, consumer cooperatives, and the like. In other words, where a special law exists for the creation of an entity other than the three traditional forms, the activity of a prescribed entity is off limits for LLC purposes. Still, this leaves much to the entrepreneurial imagination of the founders, owners, and managers of an LLC.

In this chapter, we want to discuss the general characteristics of an LLC in terms of the three traditional forms. We will limit our discussion to the operational features — the day-to-day affairs — of the traditionals. For this, we assume that the traditionals are in being and are operating successfully. All we want to do is to point out why we believe an LLC is a unique entity of its own. We do want to stress, however, that an LLC is not a substitute for traditional forms. It is merely another option for conducting business in a responsible way.

In our chapter heading, we refer to an LLC as a "hybrid" entity. This description is a little misleading. An LLC is not a homogenized hybrid of all the features of the three traditionals. Instead, it is a hybrid combination of *selected features* only. Otherwise, as a homogenized hybrid, all the traditionals would convert to an LLC. Business, tax, and legal abuses would then run rampant. The reality is that an LLC must take its proper place in the business-for-profit world.

Not a Corporation

Although an LLC has certain limited liability features like that of a corporation, it is not a corporation . . . and cannot be. There are statutory reasons for this.

All 50 states plus the District of Columbia have incorporation laws of their own. Incorporation is required for specific business activities as defined by each state. Separately, also, each of the 50 states (plus D.C.) has an LLC law. Common sense tells you that where there's a corporation law and also an LLC law, any proposed new entity cannot be both at the same time. You are either a corporation or an LLC: one or the other.

IRS Regulation § 301.7701-3(a) prescribes that—

*A business entity that is **not** classified as a corporation under § 301.7701-2(b)(1), (3), (4), (5), (6), (7), or (8)* . . . [is an eligible entity for electing LLC status].

The cross-reference to Regulation 2(b) etc. means that certain entities are *per se* corporations. That is, their characteristics are such that they are intrinsically corporations, whether the founders want them to be or not.

An intrinsic (or per se) corporation has such universal features as: (1) limited liability; (2) centralized management; (3) free transferability of ownership interests; and (4) continuity of life (indefinitely). An insurance company, for example, is inherently a corporation. So, too, is a banking organization, an electric utility, an automobile firm, a TV network, and so on.

A per se corporation is a profit-seeking entity of the C-type (as opposed to the S-type: explained later). As such, a per se corporation is not permitted to elect out of its corporate status to become an LLC. There is an obvious reason for this prohibition. A for-profit corporation issues securities (stock, bonds, notes of indebtedness, etc.) which are sold to the public for raising capital. With very limited exceptions, all corporate securities are required to be registered with state and federal authorities before being offered to the public. Were a corporation to become an LLC, it would lose its security ratings altogether. Then, its potential for raising large amounts of capital for operating needs would be curtailed.

Where Confusion Arises

Founders and owners of LLCs often like to think of themselves as corporations for capital-raising purposes, but not as corporations for state and federal regulatory purposes. This cannot be.

Functionally and fundamentally, an LLC is an association of limited liability members. Instead of paying membership dues with voting rights attached, membership *interests* are issued. Attached to these interests are managerial rights (which automatically include voting rights). Each and every LLC member must have some managerial right in the operation of the business, in order to validate the limited liability concept.

Now, here's where corporation versus LLC confusion arises. Under federal tax regulations, an association of LLC members can elect to be treated as a corporation for *income tax purposes* only. Such an election, if made, does **not** convert an LLC into a per se corporation for securities-issuing purposes. It is an income taxation election: not a securities election. Let us explain.

One of the little known secrets in state laws on LLCs is the stumbling into securities law violations. Among the traditional items defined as a security (subject to registration and regulation) are certain interests in an LLC. Under California law, for example, a "security" is defined as—

> *Any . . . interest in a limited liability company and any class or series of such interests (including any fractional or other interest in such interest),* **except** *a membership interest in a limited liability company in which the person claiming this exception can prove that* **all members are actively engaged in the management** *of the limited liability company;* [California Corporations Code § 25019: *Security*]. [Emphasis added.]

This example state law is further confirmation of the fact that an LLC cannot convert to a per se corporation by simply electing to be income taxed as a corporation. Only per se corporations can issue and sell securities. Many registered securities have voting rights. None, however, have managerial rights. As emphasized in the citation above, all LLC members must have the right to actively participate in the management of the business. This is not the case with ordinary shareholders in a corporation.

Why would an association of LLC members elect to be income taxed as a corporation?

Answer: Good question. The profits of a per se corporation are double-taxed. They are income taxed at the corporate level, and are income taxed again at the dividends level to individual shareholders. Accept it or not, this double taxation is the perfect mechanism for isolating ordinary shareholders from any personal liability for misdeeds of the corporation or of its officers and managers. We call this feature: *accounting isolation* (the bullet-proof legal shield). That is, attention focuses on the capital base of the corporate entity.

So important is this accounting isolation of corporate taxation that we present a depiction of it in Figure 1.1. The depicted isolation is also necessary for an LLC to maintain the limited personal liability of its members. We ask, however, is there a better way of

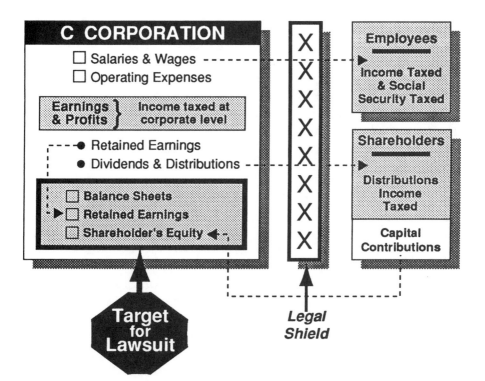

Fig. 1.1 - The "Accounting Isolation" Role of a Corporate Tax Return

achieving accounting isolation without being double taxed? Yes, there is. Perhaps via an S corporation?

S Corporation Features

For federal tax purposes, there are two types of corporations. There is a C-type and an S-type. The letters "C" and "S" get their identification from Subchapter C and Subchapter S, respectively, of the Internal Revenue Code. Subchapter C is titled: *Corporate Distributions and Adjustments*; Subchapter S is titled: *Tax Treatment of S Corporations and Their Shareholders*. For ease of distinction, it is helpful to think of a C corporation as the premier form of doing business anywhere in the U.S. and anywhere in the world. It has unlimited territorial reach, unlimited diversity of activities, unlimited access to capital, unlimited number and type of shareholders, and . . . unlimited life. The term "unlimited" is relative. Every political division of the world globe has its own franchise rules and regulations and its own securities offering laws.

An S corporation, on the other hand, is a domestic corporation with a limited number of shareholders. Only one class of stock can be issued. It is an *elective* corporation requiring the unanimous consent of all of its shareholders. If the prescribed election process is not made, or if it is deficient in any procedural respect, the shareholder entity automatically becomes a C corporation. Whether C or S, each is a completely separate tax accounting entity of its own. The formality of the two corporate tax returns and their backup records are near-identical. Thus, the financial accounting isolation of an S corporation provides the limited liability equivalent of a C corporation. This is a point worthy of note by LLC members.

There is one clear advantage of an S corporation over a C corporation. There is no double income taxation. All profits and losses are passed directly through to the individual shareholders in proportion to their shareholding interests. Each shareholder pays income tax on the distributive share of the S corporation income that he receives. The S corporation itself pays no income tax . . . at the federal level. This, too, is a point worthy of note by LLC members.

For this pass-through tax benefit, certain shareholder restrictions apply. First off, the number of shareholders is limited to 75. Secondly, all shareholders must be individual persons who are either U.S. citizens or U.S. residents. And, thirdly, only one class of stock can be issued (which must have voting rights). The stock is required to be registered but is limited to private sales only. No public offering of S stock is authorized. For these reasons and others, an S corporation is also referred to as a small business corporation (the "S" for "small").

Not all 50 states recognize the S corporation status. Many of those that do impose a modified corporate franchise tax. Take California, for example. Its C corporation tax rate is a flat 8.8%. Its S corporation tax rate is also flat, but at 1.5%. Thus, under some state franchise rules, the fact that S corporations pay a small income tax forces the shareholders to maintain an adequate capital base via balance sheets and net worth statements.

At this point we ask, is there a better LLC option than electing to be taxed as an S corporation? Yes, there is. If there are two or more LLC members, they can elect to be taxed as a partnership.

Partnership Features

A partnership is any two or more persons who subscribe to a partnership agreement to conduct their active business affairs in partnership form. Unlike an S corporation, a partnership issues no shares of stock. It issues partnership interests, similar to LLC interests. Theoretically, there is no upper limit to the number of partners that can be members of a partnership. But when the number reaches 100 or more, the partnership interests become fractioned and subfractioned to the point where the fractional interests begin to take on the investor role of shares in a corporation. When this happens, the IRS can disregard the partnership arrangement and require that the association of interest holders be taxed as a C corporation. The partnership can, however, elect to be treated as a *Large Partnership* (with over 100 partners) whose interests can be publicly traded on established and secondary securities markets.

In federal tax parlance, a bona fide partnership is a Subchapter K entity. The "K" refers to that batch of 36 separate and specific sections in the Internal Revenue Code titled: ***Partners and Partnerships***. The first of these 36 sections is Section 701: ***Partners, Not Partnership, Subject to Tax***. This lead-off section reads—

A partnership as such shall not be subject to income tax. Persons carrying on business as partners shall be liable for income tax only in their separate capacities.

In other words, a partnership acts as a conduit through which tax consequences flow to the individual partners. A portion of the partnership income, equal to the partner's distributive share, is then reported and taxed on each partner's separate tax return. The partners are liable for tax on the partnership income regardless of whether the income is distributed or retained as capital. If the partnership agreement lacks economic substance (meaning: pursuing abusive tax practices), it can be disregarded. The partnership items must be treated on each partner's separate return in a manner that is consistent with their treatment on the partnership return. Although the partnership itself pays no income tax, it does file a ***Return of Income*** return (Form 1065).

The general concept above is portrayed in Figure 1.2. The partnership agreement prescribes the relative amounts of profit sharing, loss sharing, debt sharing, liability sharing, and ownership of capital among the various partners.

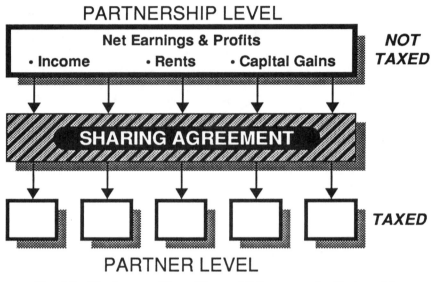

Fig. 1.2 - The Income "Pass Through" Concept of a Partnership

A partnership may consist of two liability-type partners: general and limited. A general partner is personally liable for all partnership debts, and is also jointly and severally liable for the misdeeds of associated general partners. A general partner has managerial control over the enterprise, which may be shared among other general partners. Part of this control includes a sharing of entity liabilities. A general partnership is composed only of general partners, which are relatively few in number. As owners of a business, GPs tend to be prudent and responsible for their actions.

A limited partner is one whose personal liability for partnership debts is limited to the amount of money or other property that he contributed to the partnership venture. For this limited liability, said partner has no managerial rights, but he does have distributive sharing rights to the extent of his capital contributions. A limited partnership is composed of at least one general partner and one or more limited partners.

Some states have enacted a limited liability partnership (LLP) law. Generally, a partner in an LLP is not personally liable for the debts of the LLP, nor for those LLP debts that might be assumed by any other partner. Nor is an LLP partner liable for the acts or omissions of any other partner, solely by reason of being a partner. Presumably, the management of an LLP is by one or more partners who agree to do so, in exchange for "guaranteed payments" for their services. By such payments, at least one partner is responsible for the ordinary business debts of the LLP. Some one has to be operationally responsible in a partnership.

Analogous wise, an LLC of two or more members is more like that of an LLP than either a general partnership or a limited partnership. There is a fundamental difference, however. In an LLC, each member has managerial rights on his/her/its own. This is analogous to each LLC member having his own proprietorship form of business. One or more LLC members, by informed consent in writing, can relinquish his/their managerial rights to one or more other LLC members.

Proprietorship Features

A proprietorship is a one-person beehive of business activity. One person owns the business 100%. He contributes all necessary capital, property, and services to keep the business afloat and solvent at all times. He is the owner-manager; he does all the buying of (and paying for) equipment, materials, and supplies; employs others as employees, contractors, and consultants. He can use any fictitious business name that he wants so long as no one else has chosen the same name. As a safeguard against the duplication of dba (doing business as) business names, each proprietorship owner files a *Fictitious Business Name Statement* with the Clerk's office of the county within which the business operates. Depending on the particular state in question, the statement is filed every five years or so. There is no simpler way to start up and run a business than in sole proprietorship form.

The weakness of a sole proprietorship is that the personal assets of the owner, outside of the business operation, are fully exposed to mischievous lawsuits. Business liability insurance can be purchased, but such insurance can become very expensive (particularly for construction, transportation, manufacturing, and similar small businesses). For many sole proprietors, a single-member LLC is attractive.

A sole proprietor, whether an LLC or not, files a business tax return known as Schedule C (Form 1040): *Profit or Loss from Business* and/or Schedule F (Form 1040): *Profit or Loss from Farming*. If there is a net profit from Schedule C or Schedule F, there is a second tax to pay. It is called: *Self-Employment Tax* (Schedule SE). This is not a second income tax; it is a social security and medicare tax similar to that imposed on managers and employees of other entity businesses. Nevertheless, it is a second tax to pay on an individual's personal service income. For free-wheeling LLC entrepreneurs, the self-employment tax is a "hot button" issue. They try to escape it, but are restrained by material participation rules which we discuss in Chapter 10.

Not a Business Trust

Though not ordinarily the case, a trust can be thought of as a business entity similar in many respects to a limited liability partnership. [Keep in mind at this point that we are discussing **business trusts**: not gratuitous or family trusts.] The trustee (or board of trustees) takes on the management role of a general partner. The beneficiaries of the trust are like limited partners. They contribute capital or property, called: *contributory interests*, but do not participate in the management process. In exchange for their contributory interests, they receive beneficial rights which include a prorata share of the income of the trust. Like a partnership, a business trust is generally not taxed at the entity level. However, if such a trust intentionally retains income, it is entity taxed.

Although a trustee may be a holder of one or more units of contributory interests, it is best that he be independent of such ownership interests. He should be a hired trustee, subject to replacement for malfeasance or other irresponsible conduct. The independence of a trustee is relevant because business trusts are subject to "prohibited transaction" rules. A trust is not a piggy bank, private lender, or payer of personal debts for the contributing interests. But if the trust engages in prohibited transactions or retains otherwise distributable income, it is taxed as though it were a C corporation.

Holders of contributory interests, while not taxed at the time of creating the business trust, are income taxed on all income passed through to them. Here, contributory interest holders are much like shareholders in a corporation. They are passive investors and, therefore, are not personally liable for the debts of the trust nor for the misdeeds of management. An LLC, by contrast, requires that all contributing members be active participants by "management sharing" in the entity business. Consequently, it is unlikely that an LLC could be legally formulated in trust form.

The only currently authorized business trusts under the Internal Revenue Code are—

- Real Estate Investment Trusts (REITs)
  — Code Secs. 856 through 860.

- Real Estate Mortgage Investment Conduits (REMICs)
  — Code Secs. 860A through 860G.

- Financial Asset Securitization Investment Trusts (FASITs)
  — Code Secs. 860H through 860L.

All of these authorized business trusts are off limits for an intended LLC entity. Why?

Because Regulation § 301.7701-4(a): ***Ordinary Trusts***, points out that an arrangement will be treated as a trust ONLY—

If it can be shown that the purpose of the arrangement is to vest in trustees responsibility for the protection and conservation of the property [trust assets] *for beneficiaries who cannot share in the discharge of this responsibility and, therefore, are not associates in a joint enterprise for the active conduct of a trade or business for profit.*

In other words, the fundamental concept of an ordinary trust is that, because the beneficiaries themselves contribute no property interests, they cannot participate in trust management. In contrast, the fundamental ingredient of an LLC as an entity is that there be one or more members **all** of whom share in the management responsibility for conducting business for profit.

Summary of LLC Features

The nearest analogous entities to an LLC are limited partnerships and S corporations. Both are "pass through" entities, meaning: no double income taxation. This same pass-through feature applies to an LLC. The entity net profit or loss is shared proportionately among its members, who report and pay the tax thereon in their separate capacities. Whereas a limited partnership is designated by the abbreviation "LTD", an S corporation by "INC", an LLC is indicated by "LLC". For example, "Mountain Bikes, LLC."

In an LLC, no single member is personally liable for the debts of the entity, nor for the misdeeds of other LLC members. This is similar to that of an S corporation . . . with an LLC difference. It will take a moment for us to explain.

In a limited partnership, the general partner can be held personally liable. In most such cases, however, the general partner is a C-type corporation for the sole purpose of isolating him from such personal liability. In contrast, all LLC members have management rights; as such, each is called a *member-manager*. Each member-manager has operational authority comparable to that of a general partner. The net effect is a form of consensus management as depicted in Figure 1.3.

With respect to the number of persons who can become LLC members, there is no statutory limit. The same applies to a limited partnership. In the case of an S corporation, no more than 75 shareholders are allowed. For an LLC, there is a practical limit:

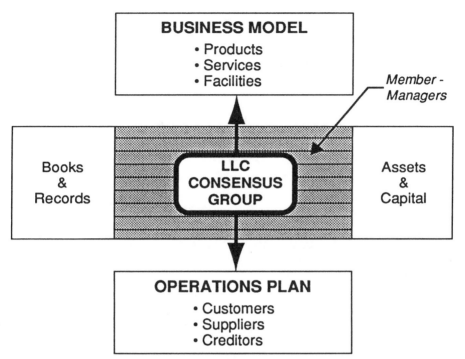

Fig. 1.3 - Concept of "Consensus Management" Among LLC Members

order of 5 to 15, but certainly no more than 25 or 30. The minimum ownership interest in an LLC with management rights is 1%. Thus, if there were 100 LLC members each with a 1% ownership interest, that would be 100 managers! No business works well with so many bosses. Would you not agree? So, there has to be some practical limit to the number of LLC participating members.

As to the type of persons (individuals or entities) who can be LLC members, there are no restrictions. Similarly, for limited partnerships. In either an LLC or a limited partnership, a member can be—

(i)   a corporation
(ii)   an active individual
(iii)   a passive individual
(iv)   a partnership

     (v)   an exempt organization
     (vi)   a nominee
     (vii)   a trust
     (viii) an estate
     (ix)   an LLC

By contrast, the membership of an S corporation is severely restricted: no corporations, no partnerships, no foreign entities, no nonresident aliens. The issuance of only one class of stock (privately placed) accounts for the many restrictions in S membership.

All entities need startup and operating capital in the form of money and property. When property is contributed, the issue of its being appreciated property (above its personal acquisition cost) or debt-encumbered property comes up. Any debt encumbrance on contributed property remains the personal liability of the contributor, unless other members agree to share and adjust their own tax basis in their separate membership accounts. Otherwise, if a contributor's debt-encumbered property exceeds his personal adjusted tax basis in that property, the contribution is a tax reportable event outside of the entity's own accounting processes. Whether forming an LLC, a limited partnership, or an S corporation, it is not an opportunity to foist upon other members the prior personal debt obligations of a high-roller contributor.

2

FORMING AN LLC

There Are Four Steps In The Formation Of An LLC. First, There Is Need To Select A Name And "Reserve It" With The Secretary Of State In Which You Intend To Do Business. Next, There Is Need For An Organizational Meeting To Designate Who Among The Participants Shall Be The "Organizer" For Filing ARTICLES OF ORGANIZATION. Third, There Is A "Statement Of Information" Designating The Principal Office Where Records Will Be Kept, Names Of Managers And Members, And Agent For Service Of Legal Process. Fourth Is An OPERATING AGREEMENT Which Only LLC Members Have The Power To Adopt, Alter, Or Amend.

The formation of a Limited Liability Company (LLC) comes under state law: not under federal law. As of April 1, 1997, all 50 states and the District of Columbia have enacted LLC statutes. The statutes vary to some degree, depending on each state's own legal practices for dealing with business activities and citizen complaints that arise from them. For this reason, it is wise to think always that the legal aspects of an LLC are a state jurisdictional matter . . . exclusively. Federal jurisdiction comes into play only when LLC income tax returns are filed.

Since the formation of an LLC is a legal process, the question arises: Which state law? It is that state within which the LLC's principal place of business is intended to be conducted. It's the state of the "home office" of the LLC operation. Once formed in one state, a domestic LLC is reciprocally recognized in other states for legal and business purposes. Foreign LLCs, however, require separate registration in every separate state in which they operate.

For practical reasons and for instructional consistency, we need to select one set of LLC statutes (among the 51) on which to base our procedural discussions. We choose California. Since the 1960s, California has been the most populated state of the nation. It has a diversity of businesses: small, medium, large, and global. It has lots of laws . . . and lots of litigation. It enacted its *Limited Liability Company Act* on September 30, 1994. The Act is codified as Title 2.5 of the California Corporations Code (CCC).

Accordingly, in this chapter, based on California law, we want to step you through the formation and confirmation process of an LLC. Our focus is strictly on the legal aspects of the process, before ever filing any LLC tax returns. When particularly instructive, we'll cite specific sections of the 48,000-word California LLC law. We do this to impress on you that an LLC involves more legal technicalities than you may have been led to otherwise believe. If ever your personal liability as an LLC member is legally challenged, you and your colleagues must show good faith in compliance with all state laws under which your LLC is formed. Any material failure to do so could pierce that "limited liability" protective shield which you so fervently cherish.

Contact Secretary of State

For the state where you intend your LLC principal office to be, your first task is to contact that state's Secretary of State. All states have such an office in the capital city of its state. The functions of the Secretary of State are those of a law clerk and administrator for business filings, election matters, state archives, and certification of official documents. For procedural matters re LLCs, the Secretary of State is THE OFFICE to contact. You can do so by Internet, fax, phone, or mail. When you do, direct your inquiry to its *Limited Liability Company Unit*. If you are uncertain as to how best to make contact, phone the local office of your state's assemblymember.

When making contact with your Secretary of State, what do you ask for? You ask for all pertinent forms, instructions, and fees for forming an LLC in your state. All you really want to know, initially, are the proper forms to file to legitimize your LLC. Large states like California will send you back a Forms Packet chock full of instructions and information. For example, California's Secretary of State will provide such documents as—

- Articles of Organization (for newly organized LLCs)
- Articles of Organization-Conversion (from a non-LLC)
- Amendment of Articles of Organization
- Restated Articles of Organization
- Statement of Information (re managers and owners)
- Designation of Agent for Service of Process
- Service of Process on LLC

. . . and so on

On the back of each LLC form, there are preprinted instructions. For example, on Form LLC-1: *Articles of Organization*, the instructions to Item 1 read, in part—

Enter the name of the limited liability company. The name shall contain the words "Limited Liability Company," or the abbreviations "LLC" or "L.L.C." as the last words in the name. The words "Limited" and "Company" may be abbreviated to "Ltd." and "Co.," respectively. . . . (Section 17052).

Section 17052 is the applicable portion of the Limited Liability Company Act in the California Corporations Code. The express title of that section is: *Company name; recordation of instruments; effect.* In other words, the official LLC forms give you a synopsized version of what the state law is. For more specifics, you need to have access to the LLC law itself.

Your State's LLC Law

With or without like-minded colleagues, if you intend to form an LLC or to become a member of an existing one, prudence suggests that you acquire some familiarity with your state's LLC law. Sure, you could go to an attorney and have him or her guide you. But you'll not gain any "hands-on" knowledge this way. Attorneys, by training, are not very helpful in the exploratory, formulative, startup, and operational phases of a business. You'll need them later when binding contracts are required, and when litigative issues come up. For now, it is better that you do the paralegal research on your own.

In any manner that you can, get access to a complete copy of your state's LLC law. Search the web for legal sites and law book publishers. If frustration sets in, call the Law Librarian or Bar Association in the county where you reside. Ask for publisher references on law books that you can buy. Then write, phone, or e-mail the publisher for a compact edition (or an annotated edition with case citations) of LLC law. You want a printed and bound text in your hand that you can browse through and read and reference from time to time. Expect to pay $50 to $100 for such a text. You have no intention of becoming an LLC legal expert; you just want to become familiar first-hand, with what the law is all about.

Browse through the LLC portion, and flag the content listing for each chapter. For example, California's LLC Chapter 2 is titled: *Formation*. Its chapter contents are listed as follows:

Section
17050 — Formation; requirements.
17051 — Articles of organization; contents.
17052 — Company name; recordation of instruments; effect.
17053 — Certificate of reservation of name; fee; issuance.
17054 — Amendment of articles of organization; filing; etc.
17055 — Certificate of correction; contents; execution; etc.
17056 — Execution of documents; resubmission; etc.
17057 — Maintenance of records; agent for service of process.
17058 — Information required to be maintained.
17059 — Operating agreement; power to adopt; alter; etc.
17060 — Statement of information.
17061 — Service of process.
17062 — Filing of instruments; date of filing.

There are 15 chapters of California LLC law. There is a total of 105 sections comprising approximately 48,000 words of text.

Obviously, familiarity does not mean reading and memorizing every one of the 48,000 words. Some chapters can be glanced at and bypassed altogether. For example, the chapters on dissolution, foreign LLCs, class actions, conversions, and mergers are not of priority interest when forming and launching a newly organized domestic LLC. In contrast, those chapters on general provisions, members, management, finance, and so on, are vital to understanding the legal underpinnings of the LLC undertaking.

Go through and highlight those sections prescribing the general provisions and general limitations of an LLC. For example, under California law, Section 17050(B) states—

A limited liability company shall have one or more members.

Thus, in California, as in most other states, single member LLCs are permitted. The law, however, is written with multiple members in mind. No upper limit on number of members is specified. Depending on the type of business intended, and the amount of capital needed to run the business, there is some practical limit to every LLC membership. Each person who has a "capital interest" in the LLC (by contributing money, property, or services) is a part owner thereof. Having too many part owners, each with a voice in management, is just not going to work well.

What kind of business can your LLC engage in? Answer: California Section 17002: *Business activity; limitations*, states—

*Subject to any limitations contained in the articles of organization and to compliance with other applicable laws, a limited liability company may engage in **any lawful business activity**, except the banking business, the business of issuing policies of insurance and assuming insurance risks, or the trust company business.* [Emphasis added.]

Except for the exceptions, "any lawful business activity" is quite broad. In fact, it is too broad. For practical reasons, every LLC should narrow its focus to some reasonably achievable business domain. Even though the law may imply so, you can't do everything. Common sense must prevail.

The Essence of Formation

Section 17050 of California LLC law is titled: *Formation; requirements*. Therein lies the essence of forming an LLC. Other states, we're sure, have identical (or nearly so) requirements.

The Section 17050 (**a**) reads—

> *In order to form a limited liability company, one or more persons shall execute and file articles of organization with, and on a form prescribed by, the Secretary of State and, either before or after the filing of the articles of organization, the members shall have entered into an operating agreement. The person or persons who execute and file the articles of organization may, but need not, be members of the limited liability company.*

Note that two separate documents are required: (1) Articles of Organization, and (2) an Operating Agreement. Note that articles of organization are to be on a form prescribed by the Secretary of State. If you've followed our advice earlier, you would have in your hands such a form, or would have requested it. This form, in California, is designated as LLC-1: *Limited Liability Company; Articles of Organization.* We'll discuss the contents of this form, in full, shortly below.

Meanwhile, it is significant to note that there is no prescribed form for an operating agreement. Why? Because it is up to the LLC members themselves to prepare their own operating agreement form. This is what is meant by "either before or after" the filing of articles of organization . . . *the members **shall have** entered into an operating agreement.* At some point, therefore, all prospective members have to get together at an organizational meeting and agree on the elements of their modus operandi.

Our position is that prospective members should get together **before** filing articles of organization. They need to thrash out among themselves the pros and cons of an LLC; the general provisions and limitations of their state's LLC law; the extent and content of its official forms; the type of business (or businesses) they propose to get into; the initial amount of capital needed;

whether or not "certificates of membership" will be issued; the assignment of managerial tasks; the outlining of voting procedures and rights; the designation of books, records, and accounts to be kept; the selection of a company name; and so on. We depict in Figure 2.1 what some of the agenda items might be, for constituting an organizational meeting.

The meeting should be conducted in a business-like manner. Minutes should be taken and printed up for subsequent distribution to all attendees. The "meeting" may consist of two, three, or more consecutive sessions and still be classed as an organizational meeting. The objective should be: (1) an *outline* of the operating agreement; (2) a tentative decision on a company name; and (3) the designation of an "organizer" who is to prepare, execute, file, and advance the filing fee for the Articles of Organization.

Note that we say a "tentative" decision on a company name. As per Section 17052(c), the name—

Shall not be a name that the Secretary of State determines is likely to mislead the public and shall not be the same as, or resemble so closely as to tend to deceive the name of any LLC that has filed articles of organization . . ., or any name that is under reservation for another LLC.

Section 17053 specifies that—

Any applicant may, upon payment of the fee prescribed . . ., obtain from the Secretary of State a certificate of reservation of any name not prohibited . . . for a period of 60 days.

The point we are making is that any member-agreed company name is only tentative. It is so until the Secretary of State accepts it and reserves it by issuing a certificate. You want to nail down your LLC name before actually filing its articles of organization.

Articles of Organization; Contents

The legitimacy of an LLC is affirmed by the filing of its Articles of Organization, and the acceptance of them by the Secretary of

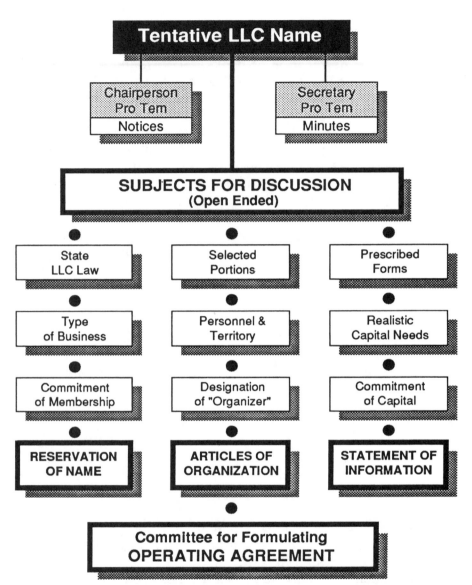

Fig. 2.1 - LLC Meeting for Preliminary Discussion & Concensus

State. This is the function of the designated "Organizer" listed in Figure 2.1. In California, the law on point is Section 17050(**c**). This section reads—

The existence of a limited liability company begins upon the filing of the articles of organization. For all purposes, a copy of the articles of organization duly certified by the Secretary of State is **conclusive evidence** *of the formation of a limited liability company and prima facie evidence of its existence.*

Section 17051 outlines the contents of the Articles document: name, purpose, type of business, management, termination, agent for service, etc. In California, all of the statutory content required is preprinted on its Form LLC-1 (cited earlier). This official form is self-explanatory, especially after reading its instructions on the back. A bold headnote there says—

DO NOT ALTER THIS FORM
Type or legibly print in black ink.

If other information is to be provided, it is to be made on separate attached pages. The executed form itself, plus a $70 filing fee, is all that California wants.

If you intend to become an LLC in a state which does not provide a preprinted Articles of Organization form, request its Secretary of State to provide you with a sample of what it wants. At least ask for its statutory requirements so that you (with an attorney) can make up your own form.

Because the California Form LLC-1 is statutorily complete, instead of going through its contents item by item, we present a condensed version of it in Figure 2.2. Note that in the upper right-hand corner, there is blank space for entering a **File #**_____. Once assigned, this number is used on all correspondence and filings between the LLC and the Secretary of State. Do not confuse this number with any Tax I.D. (Federal or State) that must be used when filing tax returns.

Item 3 in Figure 2.2 requires that either the name of an individual, or the name of a corporation, be entered as the Agent for Service of (legal) Process. Often this is an attorney or legal firm, though it could be any designated member of the LLC. This is your tip-off that being an LLC does not exonerate the LLC or its members from litigative actions.

	State of California Secretary of State ◆ LIMITED LIABILITY COMPANY ARTICLES OF ORGANIZATION	File # _____ ⌐ Space for ⌐ State Certification ⌐
STATE SEAL Filing Fee $____		

1.	Name of company ....
2.	Purpose of company (all preprinted; no changes allowed)
3.	Name of agent for service of process: ☐ Individual .... ☐ Corporation
4.	California address of agent: ....
5.	Company will be managed by: **(Check One)** ☐ one manager ☐ single member LLC ☐ more than one manager ☐ all LLC members
6.	Other matters to be included. Attach separate pages.
7.	Number of pages attached ....
8.	Type of business ....
9.	DECLARATION: by person who executes instrument. _Signature of Organizer_ _Type or Print Name_ Date _____
10.	RETURN TO: Name Company Address

Sec/State Form LLC - 1

Fig. 2.2 - Condensed Version of California "Prescribed" Form LLC-1

Item 6 permits other matters to be set forth on separate pages, to be made part of the certification process. The instructions encourage the inclusion of the latest date or event on which the LLC is to dissolve. The implication is that an LLC shall not have indefinite life, like that of a corporation.

Item 9 is a Declaration by the Organizer who is executing and signing the Articles of Organization. The instructions stress that only an _original signature_ (not a facsimile) is acceptable by the Secretary of State. As indicated previously in Section 17050(a), the signature of the organizer need not be that of a member or manager of the LLC. However, our position is that the organizer should be an LLC member. This way, he or she has more direct feel for the reality of documentation and formalities required.

Statement of Information

Within 90 days after the filing of Articles of Organization, California law requires the filing of a statement of information *on a form prescribed by the Secretary of State.* Said prescribed document is **Form LLC-12**: *Limited Liability Company: Statement of Information.* As with the LLC-1, self-explanatory instructions are on the back of Form LLC-12. The leadoff instructions tell you that said form is required biennially (every two years) after its initial filing.

The primary purpose of the Statement of Information is to keep the Secretary of State's LLC files up to date with respect to the—

1. Agent for service of process,
2. Principal business activity,
3. Office(s) for maintenance of records, and
4. Names and addresses of all members, managers, and CEOs

   (if any) . . . on attached pages (as necessary).

Persons authorized to execute and sign Form LLC-12 "shall be" any manager (or CEO), attorney in fact, or any member designated by majority vote of the LLC governing body. The declarant (executing agent) attests that—

This statement is true, correct, and complete.

By innuendo in the instructions to Form LLC-12, the declaration of truthfulness and completeness includes Section 17057: *Offices for maintenance of records.* This section reads—

Each limited liability company **shall continuously maintain** *in this state* [California] *each of the following:*

(a) An office at which shall be maintained the records required by Section 17058.

(b) An agent in this state for service of process on the limited liability company. [Emphasis added.]

We're not sure that you sense the legal significance of what we've just presented to you. If not, we depict in Figure 2.3 what we believe to be the jugular vein of an LLC operation. Like any business entity, an LLC **is subject to** litigative attack by any customer, supplier, lender, or member who becomes disgruntled or dissatisfied in his/her/its dealings with the LLC entity. A reasonable cause would exist if there is any failure to comply with ALL of the elements of Section 17058 (of California law).

Information Required to be Maintained

Section 17058 is titled: *Information required to be maintained at office.* The term "at office" means the principal, head, home, or central office of the LLC. If the required information is scattered among various members, managers, and agents, the arrangement would be "out-of-sync" with the statutory requirement for California. We are sure that other states insist similarly.

Because of the importance of Section 17058, we want to cite it, essentially in full. It reads (with emphasis added)—

(a)   Each limited liability company shall maintain at the office . . . all of the following:

(1)   A current list of the full name and last known business or residence address of each member and of each holder of an economic interest in the LLC set forth in alphabetical order, together with the contribution and the share in profits and losses of each member and holder of an economic interest.

(2)   A current list of the full name and business or residence address of each manager.

Fig. 2.3 - Potential Litigants If Mandated Records Not Maintained

*(3)   A copy of the articles of organization and **all amendments thereto**, together with any powers of attorney pursuant to which the articles of organization or any amendments thereto were executed.*

*(4)   Copies of the LLC's **federal, state, and local income tax or information returns** and reports, if any, for the **six most recent taxable years**.*

(5) A copy of the LLC's operating agreement, if in writing, and any amendments thereto . . .

*(6) Copies of the **financial statements** of the LLC, if any, for the six most recent fiscal years.*

*(7) The books and records of the LLC as they relate to the **internal affairs** of the company for at least the current and past four fiscal years.*

*(b) Upon request of an Assessor, a domestic or foreign LLC owning, claiming, possessing, or controlling **property** in this state **subject to local assessment** shall make available . . . at the office required . . . or at a place mutually acceptable to the Assessor and the LLC, a true copy of business records relevant to the amount, cost, and value of all property that it owns, claims, possesses, or controls within the county.*

The tracking, preparing, posting, and maintaining the above information — **continuously** — is a tall order. It is daunting and burdensome to an LLC whose members are cavalier, procrastinative, and indifferent to recordkeeping chores. This characteristic alone justifies the need for an explicit Operating Agreement . . . IN WRITING. Note that paragraph 17058(a)(5) above refers to such agreement as: *if in writing*. If not in writing, can't you see the finger pointing among members when responsibility questions arise, finances are low, and assets are dispersed. This is reckless exposure of your jugular vein, when legal adversaries start their drum beat and war dance.

Operating Agreement: A "Must"

Of the 105 sections of California LLC law (2001 version), only Section 17059 addresses directly the issue of an operating agreement. This is a two-sentence section comprising 46 words only. Its gist is succinctly stated in its title: *Operating agreement; power to adopt, alter, amend, or repeal; procedures*. Its first sentence reads—

*The power to adopt, alter, amend, or repeal the operating agreement of a limited liability company **shall be vested** in the members.* [Emphasis added.]

Note that no power to adopt an operating agreement is vested in an organizer, manager, agent, attorney, or other person who is not a member of the LLC. Only bona fide members (those who contribute capital) have the power to adopt, alter, amend, repeal . . . etc. It is significant to further note that the statutory wording does **not** say: "shall adopt." The wording only says: "power to adopt."

The second sentence of Section 17059 reads—

*The articles of organization **or a written** operating agreement **may prescribe** the manner in which the operating agreement may be altered, amended, or repealed.* [Emphasis added.]

This does not tell us very much other than that a written operating agreement is included in the power to adopt. But, what is an "operating agreement"? What happens if the LLC members fail to adopt an operating agreement in writing?

California Section 17001(ab) defines such an instrument as—

*Any agreement, **written or oral,** between **all** the members as to the affairs of a limited liability company and the conduct of its business in any manner not inconsistent with law or the articles of organization. . . .The term "operating agreement" may include, **without more,** an agreement between all members to organize a limited liability company pursuant to the provisions of this title* [Title 2.5: Limited Liability Companies; California Corporations Code]. [Emphasis added.]

Here's the answer to our question about failure to adopt a written operating agreement. Members may agree orally — or, they may agree *silently* — not to have such an instrument. If they so agree (not to have), they expose themselves to mandatory compliance with each and every item of the 48,000-word CCC Title 2.5! This is a legal doctrine of long standing. When given an opportunity to do something, and the response is silence, the silence is construed to mean consent to the "maximum provisions" imposed by law.

Consequently, we cannot urge too strongly that a written operating agreement be adopted by LLC members. It need not be an elaborate document. But it does need to cover the relationships between members themselves, between members and the LLC, and between the LLC and the public at large (particularly customers, suppliers, and lenders). The instrument should also include the assignment of tasks, capital requirements, recordkeeping, financial statements, tax returns, and other internal affairs which are characteristic of a well-run enterprise. For other thoughts, study our Figure 2.4.

Unlike the Articles of Organization, for which no attorney is necessary, we urge that you do engage an attorney. Engage one who is knowledgeable in LLC case law for your state, and who will not draft an instrument that is too sophisticated or too obfuscative to be comprehended fully by all members. Think of the instrument as a binding contract between serious members who intend to engage in business seriously.

Cash Starvation by Members

There is one critical area where an operating agreement can prove its worth. It is the matter of capital contributions to, shortages of, and withdrawals from company assets. Virtually every small- and medium-sized business tends to be capital starved. An LLC, with members who are fascinated with misconceptions of the limited liability concept, is particularly susceptible to the cash starvation process. A responsibly adopted operating agreement can forestall — and possibly prevent — the premature termination of an enterprise based on capital deficiencies alone. On this premise, California LLC Sections 17200 and 17201 are instructive.

Section 17200: *Capital contributions*, reads in part—

The operating agreement may provide for capital contributions of members. [Such contributions] *may be in money, property, or services, or **other obligation** to contribute money or property or to render services.* [Emphasis added.]

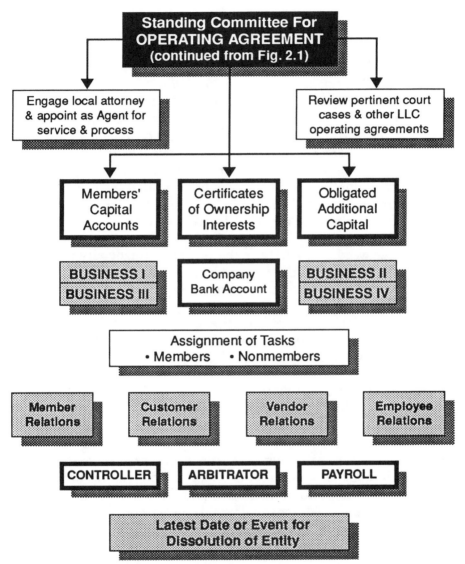

Fig. 2.4 - Indicators of the Seriousness (and Continuity) of LLC Effort

Note in the foregoing citation the term: "obligation to . . .". Said obligation is spelled out expressly in Section 17201: *Obligation to contribute cash, property, or services* (etc.). This section reads in part—

> *Subject to the terms of the operating agreement, a member is* ***not excused*** *from an obligation . . . to perform any promise to contribute cash or property or to perform services because of death, disability, dissolution, or any other reason. . . . An operating agreement may provide that the* [ownership] *interest of a member who fails to make any contributions or other payment that the member is required to make* ***will be subject*** *to specific remedies for, or specific consequences of, the failure. . . . The specific remedies or consequences may include loss of voting, approval, or other rights, loss of the member's ability to participate in the management and operations of the company, liquidated damages, or* ***a reduction of*** *the defaulting member's* ***economic rights***. [Emphasis added.]

In other words, an LLC has the power to financially discipline its own members. Failure to do so, when economic prudence requires, could be construed as prima facie evidence that the LLC is functioning as a sham.

Section 17003: ***Powers in carrying out business activities***, lists 20 paragraphs of specific LLC powers (subsections (a) through (t)). For example, subsection (d) states that an LLC has the power to—

> *make contracts and guarantees, incur liabilities, act as surety* [be responsible for its members], *and borrow money.*

Can't you sense the flood of legal actions against your LLC should it exercise its business powers without obligating all members to come forth financially? Of all the opportunistic features of an LLC, we think that failure to obligate members to maintain an adequate capital base is an LLC's most vulnerable weakness.

3

LIABILITY OF MEMBERS

Every LLC Member Can Expect Protection Against Personal Liability IF, AND ONLY IF, Certain Conditions Are Met. Among These Are: (1) Maintaining One's Agreed Share Of The LLC's Capital Base; (2) Separating, Totally, Entity Activities From Personal Activities (Otherwise, There Is ALTER EGO LIABILITY); (3) Carrying One's Load For Accuracy Of Books And Records, Including The Operating Agreement; And (4) Avoiding All Tortious Conduct (Breach Of Duty) Towards Customers And Creditors. If So Stated In The Operating Agreement, Any Member May Separately Insure Himself Against The Misdeeds Of Other Members.

There is a misconception, widely held, that by merely forming an LLC, every member thereof is insulated from all personal liability to third-party plaintiffs. This is definitely not the case. True, there is some protection against such liability **but only if** certain statutory conditions are met. The conditions are prescribed by state law, but even then the protection is limited to the extent of each member's economic interest in the LLC activity as a whole. In other words, if a member's economic interest in the LLC is $10,000, he can be held liable up to that amount . . . under most circumstances.

However, if a member engages in breach of contract, tortious acts (fraud or misrepresentation), failure to maintain his capital obligations to the LLC, or does other acts in violation of state law, no protection is afforded. The protective LLC shield is legally pierced. In this event, the member or members can be held personally liable for what might otherwise be the debts and obligations of the LLC.

The purpose of the LLC statute for the state in which you do business is to establish the compliance rules for an effective legal shield. The rules, of course, will differ from state to state. Nevertheless, the rules boil down basically to keeping certain records, maintaining adequate capital reserves, honoring contractual commitments, avoiding tortious acts, and following formalities comparable to those of a well-run corporation.

Accordingly, in this chapter, we want to continue with California law. We particularly want to focus on those statutory provisions which we think would be used foremost against you, in litigative action for probable cause. There is no better place to start than that section of California LLC law subheaded: *Liability of members* (Section 17101).

The Basic Protection Rule

Subsection (**a**) of Section 17101 provides that—

Except as provided in Section 17254 or subsection (e), **no member** *of a limited liability company* **shall be personally liable** *under any judgment of a court, or in any other manner,* **for any debt, obligation, or liability of the limited liability company,** *whether that liability or obligation arises in contract, tort, or otherwise,* **solely by reason of being** *a member of the limited liability company.* [Emphasis added.]

Except for the two exceptions, what does Section 17101(a) say? It says — between the lines — that if you as an LLC member have "deep pockets," and the LLC as an entity does not, you are protected. The mere fact that you are a member of the LLC and the fact that the LLC incurred a liability exceeding its asset and capital base, you cannot be held liable beyond your share of that base. This, at least, is a valid affirmative defense should the plaintiff establish (with credible evidence) that the LLC was run carelessly and imprudently, or violated some other law.

The legal theory here is *separable liability*. This contrasts with joint and several liability, such as in a partnership or joint venture. Consequently, separable liability is the key on which Section 17101 is premised, and on which the concept of limited liability rests. Because of its fundamental importance, we depict the separability concept for you in Figure 3.1.

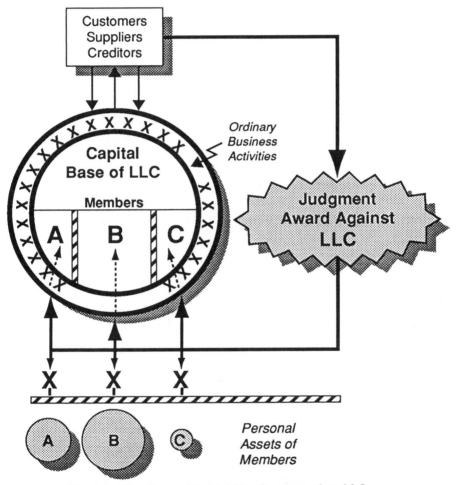

Fig. 3.1 - The Separable Liability Concept of an LLC

Let us illustrate Figure 3.1 with simple numbers. You are one of three members in an LLC. As member "A" you have a 30%

ownership interest which represents $50,000 of the LLC's capital base. The LLC is sued for some cause whereupon the plaintiff is awarded a $100,000 judgment. Your share of that judgment is $30,000 ($100,000 x 30%). It is not the full $50,000 of your economic interest in the LLC. This is because the plaintiff will get $50,000 from member "B" ($100,000 x 50%) and $20,000 from member "C" ($100,000 x 20%).

Instead, now, suppose your 30% interest represents $25,000 of the LLC's capital base. The plaintiff, again, is awarded $100,000 against the LLC. Arithmetically, your share of the liability is $30,000. But the plaintiff can only collect $25,000 from the LLC for your part. Can the plaintiff go after you personally for the $5,000 liability deficiency on your part?

Technically, No. But he will try. Knowing how aggressive trial attorneys can be, the plaintiff's attorney will hammer away at the LLC shield until some tiny pinhole appears.

The "Prohibited Distribution" Rule

How can a trial attorney pierce the LLC shield when you are protected by Section 17101(a)?

Answer: This is where the first exception to Section 17101(a) comes in. Recall that its opening clause reads— *Except as otherwise provided in Section 17254. . . .* What is this cross-reference all about?

Section 17254 is titled: ***Prohibited distributions***, etc. Its subsection (a) states primarily that—

*No distribution shall be made if, after giving effect to the distribution, **either** of the following occurs:*

*(1)   The LLC would **not be able to pay its debts** as they become due in the normal course of business.*

*(2)   The LLC's total assets would be less than **the sum of its total liabilities** plus . . . the amount that would be needed, if the LLC were to be dissolved at the time of the distribution. . . .* [Emphasis added.]

Let's go back to the $100,000 judgment liability example above. Suppose that shortly after the lawsuit was filed, you, as a 30% member, requested a distribution of $25,000 of your $50,000 capital base in the LLC. The 50% member agreed; the 20% member disagreed. After your drawdown, the company was left with enough assets to pay its ordinary debts when due [paragraph (1) above]. Now, what?

As per paragraph (2) above, your $25,000 distribution caused the company assets to fall below its total liabilities when including the $100,000 judgment. Knowing that a lawsuit had been filed, your request constitutes negligence and impropriety. Thus, you will be liable for your full 30% share of the judgment.

Now, suppose the 50% member demands distribution of his entire capital base in the LLC (around $85,000). You and the 20% member vehemently disagree. The 50% member becomes violent, pounds the table, and threatens a counter lawsuit against both of you. Reluctantly — and nervously — you both agree. Each of you has left all of your initial capital base in the LLC (totaling also around $85,000). The judgment and ordinary debts are expected to total about $150,000. Are you and your 20% colleague LLC protected? You thought so, didn't you?

Surprise! You both have compounded your negligence and impropriety. As a result, you both are treated as partners ex parte (outside of the LLC). You both now are jointly and severally liable for the $100,000 judgment *and* for the approximately $50,000 of ordinary LLC debt. The plaintiff and creditor(s) can collect from either of you or from both of you. When a matter is statutorily prohibited, as Section 17254 says, and you violate that prohibition, the LLC shield provides no protection whatsoever.

The "Agree to be Obligated" Rule

There's a second exception to the basic LLC protection rule. It is subsection (e) of Section 17101 as cross-referenced above. The subsection (e) reads—

*Notwithstanding subsection (a), **a member** of an LLC **may agree to be obligated personally for any or all** of the debts,* *obligations, and liabilities of the LLC as long as the agreement to be so obligated is set forth . . . in a written operating agreement that specifically references this subsection.* [Emphasis added.]

Why would a member *agree to be obligated* for any or all of an LLC's debts and liabilities? There are valid reasons.

Note that Section 17101(e) says "a" member. It does not say "all" members. Also note that the personal liability assumed may apply to "**any** or all" of the LLC's obligation. We're not sure of the legal interpretation of these items. Ordinary reasoning suggests that if one member assumed a specific obligation beyond his required capital base, he has insulated himself from other extraneous matters, should other members of the LLC engage in improper acts.

It is beyond us why any one member would obligate himself for all of the debts and liabilities of a multi-member LLC. If other members appear to be irresponsible in their business duties, why carry the load for all? However, if it is a two-member LLC, and one member is not carrying his load, the responsible member could assume all obligations and "vote out" the non-performing member.

Every LLC is supposed to have a capital base sufficient to cover all ordinary debts when due, plus the cost of dissolution. When there are three or more members in an LLC that is chronically "cash short," a more prudent member might agree to obligate himself for his share of any lawsuits that might arise. No matter how justified a lawsuit might be, the settlement time and judgment award are difficult to predict. Rather than worrying about collateral liability based on some quirky technicality, a member might obligate himself in advance. By doing so in writing (in the LLC's operating agreement), he can set the terms and conditions for his added obligation. Presumably, such could stave off any unconscionable lawsuit against that member. Presumably, also, the LLC protection shield would hold for that member.

The "Shall Carry Insurance" Rule

There is another statutory rule that further defines the degree of legal protection that an LLC affords. The applicable rule is subsection (d) of Section 17101. We call it the "shall carry insurance" rule. Subsection (d) reads as—

> *An LLC . . . shall carry insurance **or provide an undertaking to the same extent** and in the same amount as is required by law, rule, or regulation of this state that would be applicable to the company . . . **were it a corporation** . . . duly qualified for the transaction of intrastate business under the General Corporation Law* [of California]. [Emphasis added.]

This is not a particularly definitive requirement. We think it invites lawsuit because of its lack of specifying an overall amount (such as a percentage of gross sales), and its lack of identifying specific coverage(s). How much, and what type of insurance is adequate for an LLC? Can't you see a trial lawyer probing this matter to threads?

If there is no insurance at all carried by the LLC, you can be sure that this would be one of the causes of action in a lawsuit. Even if the defense were "an undertaking to the same extent" (as insurance), it would be a hard sell in court.

One equivalent undertaking that would likely be accepted is the "agreement to obligate" provision in subsection (e) above. Another equivalent undertaking would be a disciplinary provision in the operating agreement requiring personal liability insurance by each capital-deficient member. The insurance would be purchased and paid for by each deficient member, naming the LLC as the beneficiary of the proceeds. A nominal face-amount policy, such as $100,000, should be prescribed by the disciplinary agreement.

What is the guideline if none of the equivalent measures above is acceptable to LLC members? In this case, the manager must undertake a survey of the insurance coverage by those businesses similar to his, which are in corporate form. This is smart for two reasons. One, you cover the intent of law. And, secondly, the competitive premium rates would likely be lower for corporations than for a fully exposed LLC. Our contention is that, by being an LLC, insurers are likely to "pad" their rates. Especially so if it appears that some members consider the limited liability shield itself as being a form of insurance. Indeed, many LLC participants decline to carry any form of liability insurance in the belief that their LLC status gives them all the legal protection they need. We are sorry to have to cast cold water on any such delusion(s).

The "Alter Ego Liability" Rule

The doctrine of alter ego liability is one of long standing. It has evolved from the many abuses of closely-held entities, such as corporations, partnerships, and trusts. And, now, closely-held LLCs. The term "closely held" means five or fewer individuals owning 50% or more of the controlling interests of an entity. In these situations, the distinction between entity business and personal business is blurred and commingled. To invoke the alter ego doctrine, it has to be shown that the entity was a mere conduit for the transaction of personal business and that no separate identity of the individual and the entity really existed.

The lack of separate identity stands out starkly when there is commingling of funds, disguisement of expenditures, unrestrained drawdown of capital, poor recordkeeping, lavish travel and entertainment, and the like. Owner self-discipline in separating business from personal matters is minimal or nonexistent. The entity formulation and use of its registered name is an "ego thing" for the close owners.

Section 17101(b) does not exonerate LLC members from alter ego liability. To the contrary, it expressly states—

*A member of an LLC **shall be subject** to liability under the common law governing alter ego liability, **and shall also** be personally liable under a judgment of a court **or for** any debt, obligation, or liability of the LLC, whether that liability or obligation arises in contract, tort, or otherwise, **under the same or similar circumstances** and to the same extent **as a shareholder of a corporation** may be personally liable.* [Emphasis added.]

There is no wiggle room here. Once it can be shown that there is no distinct line of separation between the entity and one or more of its members, each such member becomes subject to personal liability. It is the de facto act or acts that count legally. For example, the operating agreement prohibits any personal transactions on company letterhead, writing company checks, or using company equipment. Nevertheless, some senior member goes ahead and makes his monthly mortgage payments on his personal home with company checks. Doing so, he has snagged the trip wire into alter ego liability. So important is this doctrine that we depict it the best we can in Figure 3.2.

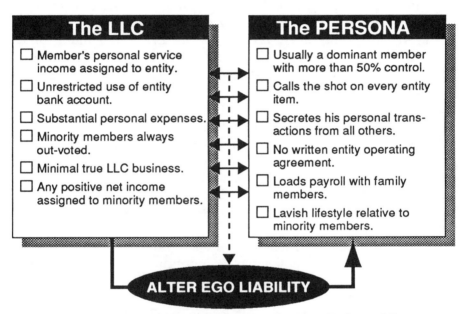

Fig. 3.2 - Elements of Indistinguishability Between Entity and Persona

It is important to be aware that if one member acquires alter ego liability, he carries his burden alone. Other members are unaffected unless they, too, ignore the separability doctrine of Figure 3.1

The "Like-a-Corporation" Standard

If you survive the separability doctrine, there are other LLC technicalities which could subject a member or members to personal liability. Most such technicalities are comparable to those of a corporation. Indeed, many LLCs structure their internal affairs "like a corporation" without the strict formalities of a corporation. The most likely first attack on this front would be the operating agreement. This instrument, functionally, is much like that of the rules and by-laws of a corporation. If an LLC truly wants legal protection, it has to act responsibly.

As a starter, California's LLC Section 17105(a): *Certificate of interest* (etc.) says—

> *The operating agreement may provide that the interest of a member or assignee in an LLC may be evidenced by a certificate of interest issued by the LLC, and make other provisions . . . with respect to the transfer of interests represented by those certificates or with respect to the form of those certificates.*

The idea of issuing "certificates of interest" representing a member's ownership in the business closely resembles the idea of shares in a corporation. True, the cited statute merely says: "*may* provide." Nevertheless, you should always count on a plaintiff's attorney demanding a copy of an LLC's operating agreement. Such a demand — called: *right of discovery* — will almost certainly open up a can of legal worms.

If no certificates of interest are issued, how does the LLC keep track of each member's separate economic interests? How meticulously are capital account records kept? Can members switch their interests back and forth among themselves and families, or freely among close friends and associates? How reliable and updated is the transactional accounting on these matters? If the operating agreement is too flexible, too unspecific, or too silent on these matters, the alter ego liability doctrine comes back into play.

A favored target for probing the adequacy of the operating agreement is Section 17202: *Profits and losses; allocation among members*. This "shall be" section reads—

> *The profits and losses of an LLC **shall be allocated** among the members, and among classes of members, in the manner provided in the operating agreement. If the operating agreement does not otherwise provide, profits and losses shall*

*be allocated **in proportion to the contributions** of each member.* [Emphasis added.]

The term "contributions" refers to the amount of money, property, and after-tax services that are dedicated irrevocably to the LLC entity, in exchange for economic interests therein.

Here's the classical legal quagmire that arises from capital accounting issues. As of on or about a certain date (of alleged misconduct), were the accounts posed prior — or subsequent — to the cause of action date? If made prior (which is good) were they made by a person of knowledge who had a duty to make the entries in a timely manner. Trying to doctor up records after a lawsuit is filed is clear admission of fault.

Retroactive Corrections Preempted

When the lawsuits against an LLC start, a flaying of finger pointing goes around. Defensive members become avid record correctors. They work feverishly to clear out adverse commentary; they substitute "corrected" versions; and they add missing or overlooked items. Those who have agreed to take on management tasks hurriedly prepare their job descriptions. The whole effort is to tighten up, retroactively, what has been a loosely run LLC.

California LLC Section 17157 preempts any retroactive reshuffling of records affecting manager and agent responsibilities. The section is titled: *Agents of the company for purposes of transacting business or affairs.* Its subsection (a) reads—

*Unless the statement referred to in subsection (b) of Section 17151 is included in the **articles of organization**, every member is an agent of the LLC for the purpose of its business or affairs, and the **act of any member** . . . for the apparent purpose of carrying on in the usual way the business or affairs of the LLC . . . **binds the LLC**, unless the member so acting has in fact no authority to act for the LLC in the particular matter, and the person with whom the member is dealing has actual knowledge of the fact that the member has no such authority.* [Emphasis added.]

Can't you see? Any after-the-fact designation of managers and delegation of authority pertaining to business and operating affairs is too late. Unless the Articles of Organization — *not* the operating agreement — provide for the management aspects of the LLC, the act or acts of every member can bind the company. Therefore, you need to know about the "Unless" clause referenced in the citation above. The reference, recall, is subsection (b) of Section 17151.

Subsection (b) of Section 17151: ***Management*** (etc.) reads primarily as—

If the LLC is to be managed by one or more managers and not by all its members, the articles of organization shall contain a statement to that effect . . . but if management is vested in only one manager, the articles of organization shall so state.

As pointed out in the preceding chapter, California provides a prescribed form for an LLC's *Articles of Organization* [recall Figure 2.2 on page 2-10]. Item 5 of that form calls to your attention the management issue. That item reads expressly as—

The limited liability company will be managed by: (check one)

☐ one manager   ☐ more than one manager

☐ all limited liability company members

☐ single member limited liability company

In other words, you have to commit your management arrangement up-front: not after-the-fact. Of course, you can always amend the Articles . . . and notify the Secretary of State when you do.

Outsourced Management Permitted

If provision is made in the Articles of Organization for management by other than all members, three benefits accrue. One, the manager or managers need not be a member of the LLC [Subsec. 17151(a)]. Two, the manager or managers need not be a natural person [Subsec. 17151(c)]. A partnership, corporation, or trust could be a manager. And, three, once management is vested in a manager or managers outside of the LLC, then—

No member, acting solely in the capacity of a member, is an agent of the LLC, nor can any member bind, nor execute any instrument on behalf of, the LLC [Subsec. 17157(b)(1)].

This sounds to us as if the outsourcing of management responsibilities of an LLC could be an advantageous way to go. Though clearly permitted by California law (and, presumably, by other states as well), whether your LLC does so or not depends on the potential for personal liability by various members. Those members or prospective members who have substantial personal assets may not want to expose those assets to the unknowns of a new or converted LLC. In such case, the idea of a Management Contract with qualified nonmembers might be appealing.

A management contract with nonmember managers would have to be an independent document of its own. It should be independent of both the Articles of Organization and the operating agreement. However, because the operating agreement is empowered by the members of the LLC (not by the Secretary of State), any decision on management policy should be set forth initially in the operating agreement. After proper proposal, discussion, and resolution by a majority of the voting member interests, an outsourced management contract can be put forth. When legally complete, such a contract can be appendaged to the operating agreement and made a part thereof, by reference. As a separate contract between the LLC and its chosen management firm, the contract is subject to litigative enforcement independent of the internal affairs of the LLC itself.

Before deciding on an outsourcing management contract, certain statutory items should be brought to the attention of all LLC members. For one, there are fiduciary duties and responsibilities of a trusted manager or managers. On this, California LLC Section 17153: *Fiduciary duties*, states—

The fiduciary duties a manager owes to the LLC and to its members are those of a partner to a partnership and to the partners of the partnership.

In other words, an outsourced manager or management firm is like a general partner in a partnership consisting of the manager (a management firm) and the LLC. This *implies* a joint and several liability relationship. Statutorily, however, outsourced managers must be extended conditional immunity from personal liability by the LLC. The relevant portion of California law here is Section 17158: *Immunity of managers.* Its statutory wording is—

*No person who is a **manager or officer** or both a manager and officer of an LLC **shall be personally liable** under any judgment of a court, or in any other manner, for any debt, obligation or liability of the LLC, whether that liability arises in contract, tort, or otherwise, **solely by reason** of being a manager or officer or both a manager and officer of the LLC.* [Emphasis added.]

In other respects, Section 17155 has particular significance of its own. Its full title is: *Indemnification of managers, members, officers, employees, or agents; insurance.* The gist here is that the operating agreement of an LLC—

may provide for the indemnification of any person, including without limitation, any manager, member, officer, employee, or agent of the LLC, against judgments, settlements, penalties, fines, or expenses of any kind incurred as a result of acting in that capacity. The LLC shall have the power to purchase and maintain insurance on behalf of any [person above].

We try to summarize the above for you in Figure 3.3. Until the management contract is either canceled or altered materially, the managers "run the show." The members function as a board of directors for policy and financial control.

No Shield for Tortious Conduct

The term "tortious" means: *of or involving a tort.* The term "tort" means: *a wrongful act, injury, or damage (not involving breach of contract) for which civil action can be brought.* These are the definitions we find in an ordinary dictionary.

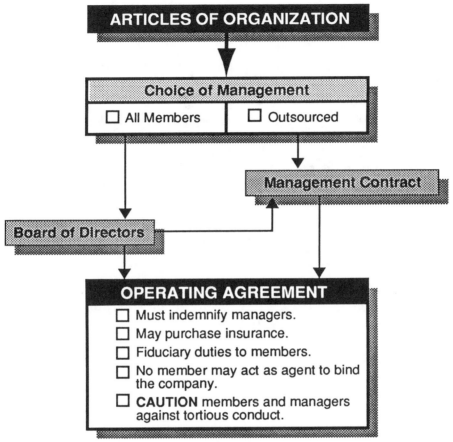

Fig. 3.3 - Features of an LLC With Outsourced Management

More specifically, tort is a legal term that covers a variety of harmful behavior. Considered "harmful" or "wrongful" is a breach of that behavior which exists by virtue of **society's expectation** regarding interpersonal conduct. Society does not expect one person to harm another person: his body, his property, his economic interests, his reputation, his privacy, his "whatever." Tort is the interference with someone else's right to life, liberty, and the pursuit of happiness. A tortious act is that which takes place beyond contract law, and that which creeps up on criminal law. Tort law is not as well codified as contract law or criminal law. Tort covers an amorphous span of human interaction generally referred to as common law.

What's our point?

It is that LLC law, of which we have cited selected California portions, is a specific form of contract law. So, too, are the statutory provisions for proprietorships, partnerships, corporations, and trusts. None of these contract-law provisions address tortious conduct. Consequently, our point is that if an LLC member engages in tortious conduct — whether knowingly or otherwise — he places himself *beyond* the protective shield of LLC law. He is then totally on his own. He has to pay for and insure against any personal liability actions out of his own pocket. He cannot expect indemnification from the LLC of which he is a member.

On this point, subsection (c) of Section 17101: *Liability of members*, is quite succinct. It states—

Nothing in this section shall be construed to affect the liability of a member to third parties for the member's participation in tortious conduct.

That's our point!

4

IRS ELECTION FORM 8832

An Eligible Entity May Elect To Be Income Taxed As A
Corporation, A Partnership, Or A Proprietorship. An
"Eligible Entity" Is Any Arrangement Of Entrepreneurial
Interests Not Statutorily Mandated To Be A Corporation.
The Election Option Is Available Whether Or Not An LLC
Is Formed. Selecting An Entity Name, And Formulating
Its Operational Characteristics Are Prerequisite To An
LLC's Effective Date. A "60-Month Rule" Discourages
"Tax Whipsawing" And "Debt Whipsawing" By Limiting
The Frequency Of Election Changes Instigated By
Aggressive Members Who Want "In" And "Out" At
Opportunistic Times Of Their Own Choosing.

Having applied for formal status as an LLC (as discussed in
Chapters 2 and 3), your next concern is the type of entity
classification you choose to be. You need to make said choice for
Federal income tax purposes. When conducting any form of
business for profit, sooner or later there will be an income tax return
to be filed. It is better that you select the form of return, rather than
letting the IRS select it for you. You have the option to do this via
Form 8832: *Entity Classification Election*.

Before you can use Form 8832, however, you must have an
entity name. This is that business name you used when you filed
your LLC Articles of Organization with the Secretary of State for
the state where your principal office will be. You also need an EIN:
Employer Identification Number. Every business tax return that

you file requires an EIN. The EIN is the **Tax ID** of the entity whether it is an employer or not. Where do you get an EIN?

From the IRS, of course. You may apply by phone or by mail. Either way, you need to have Form SS-4: *Application for Employer Identification Number.* This form not only identifies the principal owner of the business, but also its nature and type of activity, date business started, and number of employees expected (if any). Where do you get the EIN form? You may phone 1-800-829-3676 [1-800-TAX-FORM] 24 hours a day, 7 days a week. Or, you may download it from the IRS's Internet Web Site at **www.irs.gov**. While at it, also get Form 8832 and its instructions.

As a consequence of the above, our primary focus of this chapter is discussing and explaining Form 8832 to you. It is an important tax document. A copy is required to be attached to the return of each LLC member, the first taxable year in which the 8832 election is effective. The original of the form is filed with the IRS's Service Center in Philadelphia, PA (19255).

Because of new federal tax laws dealing with foreign trade, almost as much of Form 8832 is devoted to foreign LLCs as to domestic LLCs. As all national economies expand globally, some degree of engagement in foreign trade by small business is more a reality today than ever in the past. However, due to rules pertaining to "relevancy," U.S. "effectively connected" income, and the withholding of tax at source, we postpone any discussion on foreign LLCs until Chapter 12.

Apply for EIN First

Before filing Form 8832, you need to apply for an EIN: *Employer Identification Number.* As noted above, the EIN is a Tax ID of an *entity*, whether business or nonbusiness, or whether an employer or not. For this reason, we like to think of the "E" as for *Entity* rather than for "employer." Once assigned, the EIN dockets the entity from "day 1" until the entity no longer exists. The EIN is to an entity what the SSN (social security number) is to an individual person. It is a required Federal account number on all tax returns, information returns, and other communications with the IRS. One of the "other communications" is Form 8832 itself. You need an EIN in order to process the entity classification election form. You can't get very tax far without it.

As also noted above, an EIN is assigned upon preparing and filing Form SS-4: *Application for Employer Identification Number.* This form consists of about 25 entry lines and about 35 checkboxes. At line 8a, for example, there are 15 checkboxes for indicating the type of entity you choose to be. The line 8a is captioned:

> *Type of entity (Check only one box).* **Caution***: If applicant is a limited liability company, see the instructions for line 8a.*

This is your first hint that there is an interaction between Form SS-4 and Form 8832 . . . or, vice versa. Hence, you need in hand both forms at the same time.

In relevant part, the instructions for line 8a say—

> *Check the box that best describes the type of entity applying for the EIN.* **Caution***: This is not an election for a tax classification of an entity. See "Limited Liability Company (LLC)" below.*

The instructions referred to "below" say—

- *If the entity is classified as a partnership for Federal tax purposes, check the "Partnership" box.* ☐ *Partnership*

- *If the entity is classified as a corporation for Federal tax purposes, check the "Other corporation" box and write "LLC" in the space provided.* ☐ *Other corporation* _____

- *If the entity is disregarded as an entity separate from its owner, check the "Other" box and write in "disregarded entity" in the space provided.* ☐ *Other* _____

Thus, what the SS-4 instructions are saying is that, if you are an LLC, you have to decide what *tax classification* you want to be (corporation, partnership, or proprietorship) before completing line

8a. This is relatively easy to do. Because of the accounting and tax complications involved, most LLCs prefer not being taxed as a corporation. Only if you are a single-member LLC can you be taxed as a "disregarded entity." Otherwise, where there are two or more LLC members, a partnership entity is to be indicated. At this point on the SS-4, you are getting a foretaste of what Form 8832 is all about.

Other EIN Information

In other respects, Form SS-4 provides a good prognosis of what your "business model" ought to be. Various thought-provoking questions are asked. For example, you are asked—

- Reason for applying.
- Date business started or acquired.
- Closing month of accounting year.
- Principal business activity.
- Expected number of employees in the next 12 months.
- To whom are most of the products or services sold.

Other pertinent information is sought which necessitates that you read the three pages of instructions accompanying the SS-4. Said instructions are quite educational for synopsis-learning what is expected of you as a business owner, whether an LLC or other entity. Except for Federal taxation choice only, an LLC has to comply with all other tax laws that are currently in effect.

You should particularly read the SS-4 instructions at the section headed: *When to Apply for a New EIN.* Among other things, it tells you that if you become the owner of an existing business, do **not** use the EIN of the former owner. Get your own EIN. Otherwise, it would be like your using someone else's SSN on your tax return. The instruction also says: *File only one Form SS-4, regardless of the number of businesses operated or trade names used.* You are further told: *Do not apply for a new EIN if — you elected on Form 8832 to change the way the entity is taxed.*

Another "Do not apply for a new EIN" pertains to a partnership. In a partnership of any kind, members come and go. They sell, exchange, or gift their capital and profit interests (among friends, family, and associates) almost like that of stock in a corporation. When 50% or more of the total interests change hands in a 12-month period, the entity is allowed to make a short-year accounting so as to settle all old accounts. The following day, another short-year accounting resumes with new accounts, new capital, and new ownership percentages. The original EIN continues to be used, if the business operation itself has not materially changed.

Taking all of the above together, once an EIN is assigned to a partnership LLC, the same EIN can be used year in and year out, as members come and go. This is a tremendous symbolic convenience for the continuity of life of a successful LLC business.

Purpose of Form 8832

Although cited earlier, we again cite the title of Form 8832. It is: *Entity Classification Election*. Keep the word "Election" foremost in mind. If you do not exercise your election rights in a timely manner (with Form 8832), you are automatically classified — for Federal tax purposes — under Default Rules. There are three basic default rules, namely:

A. Existing entity rule
B. Domestic entity rule
C. Foreign entity rule

An entity in existence before January 1, 1997 that has already established a Federal tax classification does not need to make an election to continue that classification. This applies to domestic and foreign entities alike. If an existing entity decides to change its tax classification, the use of Form 8832 is required.

The domestic default rules require that unless Form 8832 is used, the entity is either— (1) A partnership if it has two or more members, or (2) Disregarded as an entity if it has a single owner and, therefore, is taxed as a proprietorship. Comparable default rules apply to foreign unincorporated entities.

An election using Form 8832 directs how your LLC will be *income taxed* . . . for Federal tax purposes only. The election has no effect whatever on the limited liability features prescribed by state law. Most income taxing states, but not all, follow the Federal taxation election of Form 8832. Hence, the clear purpose of Form 8832 is to elect the taxing mode of an LLC. It does nothing more, and nothing less, than this.

The instructions to Form 8832 at: *Purpose of Form*, say—

For Federal tax purposes, certain business entities are automatically classified as corporations.

They are the *per se* corporations that we discussed briefly in Chapter 1. Such corporations are organized under specific Federal or state law describing them as a corporation, incorporated, body corporate, body politic, joint-stock company, joint-stock association, insurance company, or banking institution.

Thus, all business entities that are not automatically per se corporations are "eligible entities" for purposes of Form 8832. The instructions then go on to say—

The IRS will use the information entered on this form to establish the entity's filing and reporting requirements for Federal tax purposes.

Information on the Form

If Form 8832 is an election-type form, we have to ask ourselves: "What information on the form makes it so special?" This is probably one of the simplest IRS forms that you'll ever see. In a condensed manner, we present its general contents to you in Figure 4.1. Note that it has eight distinctive stand-alone checkboxes. How much simpler can a tax form be than a series of checkboxes?

Also note that at the very first entry space, two items of information are required. These are: *Name of entity* and *EIN*. If you do not have an EIN, the instructions tell you to apply for one. We have already instructed you in this regard.

As you can see in Figure 4.1, there are five items of information required on the election form. In the sequence listed on the form, these items are:

ENTITY CLASSIFICATION ELECTION — FORM 8832

Name of entity _____ | EIN _____

1. Type of Election
   a. ☐ Initial classification when newly formed
   b. ☐ Change in current classification

2. Form of Entity
   a. ☐ Domestic association ... taxable as corporation
   b. ☐ Domestic entity ... taxable as partnership
   c. ☐ Domestic (single owner) ... taxable as proprietorship
   d. ☐ Foreign Association ... taxable as corporation
   e. ☐ Foreign entity ... taxable as partnership
   f. ☐ Foreign (single owner) ... taxable as proprietorship

3. Effective date of election ___/___/___
4. Name of person for IRS contact

_____ **5.** _____ *Phone No.* _____

Consent Statement & Signature(s)

Under penalties of perjury, I (we) -

Signature(s)	Date	Title

Fig. 4.1 - Abbreviated Arrangement of Tax Classification Election Form

1. *Type of election* (2 checkboxes)

2. *Form of entity* (6 checkboxes)

3. *Election to be effective beginning* _(m)/(d)/(yr)_

4. *Name and title of person* [for IRS to contact]

5. That person's phone number

Items 3, 4, and 5 are self-explanatory. The month, day, and year (item 3) when the election is to go into effect starts the IRS's administrative and computer tracking programs for tax compliance. However, instructions say that the effective date can not be more than 75 days prior to the filing date, nor later than 12 months after the filing date. The "filing date" is the stamped date placed on the original of the form, when actually received by the IRS Center in Philadelphia, PA.

As to the two checkboxes at item 1 (Type of election), obviously only one box can be checked. Box 1a is for a newly-formed entity electing its initial classification. Box 1b is for an existing entity changing its current classification. The clear implication is that whatever your initial election was, you can change your tax classification at a later date. When you do this with box 1b, the coordination of the effective date with the accounting-period date of the former tax classification is crucial. You want to avoid any overlapping of the required tax reporting requirements.

Checking "Form of Entity"

As self-evident in Figure 4.1, there are six checkboxes for electing one's *Form of entity* (at item 2). Obviously, only one box can be checked for each Form 8832 filed. If more than one box is checked inadvertently or intentionally, the election will be invalidated altogether. The entity default rules would then apply.

The wording at all six of the item 2 checkboxes contain a common phrase. That phrase is: *Eligible entity electing to be . . . .* Again, for emphasis, an "eligible entity" is *any* business arrangement that is **not** a per se (statutorily mandated) corporation. The importance of this concept is that Form 8832 is not the sole election province of LLC entities. In other words, a business arrangement does not have to be an LLC to be eligible to use Form 8832. Any unincorporated entrepreneur can use the form.

As to the six checkboxes on Form 8832, three are for domestic entities and three are for foreign entities. Whether domestic or foreign, the election is limited to being taxed either as a corporation, a partnership, or a proprietorship. These are the three basic conventional business forms. There is no election option to be income taxed in any other way. There is no elective provision to be taxed as a trust (whether domestic or foreign), an exempt organization, a stock or commodity trader, a nonprofit corporation, an investment company, a personal holding company, or any other specially taxed entity.

When electing to be classified "as a corporation," the entity is automatically taxed as a C corporation. This means double income taxation, first at the entity level and again at the distributee level. If you want to avoid this double taxation — who doesn't? — you must attach to Form 8832 an S corporation election form. An S corporation is a pass-through entity similar in many accounting respects to a partnership. To make the S election, use Form 2553: *Election by a Small Business Corporation.* All we can do at this point is to alert you to the existence of Form 2553 if you prefer S-status to that of a C-status corporation. Often, an "association" of small capitalists in a common venture prefers not to register under state law as an LLC. In such cases, corporate status provides the accounting and managerial discipline necessary for entity success.

When not electing to be taxed as a corporation, and there are two or more contributing capitalists, the partnership form of Federal taxation is near optimal. We think partnership taxation **is** optimal for those who have already registered (à la Chapters 2 and 3) as an LLC. For others, the limited partnership form is preferable. In a limited partnership, the general partner can be a C corporation for limiting his personal liability in the joint venture. We'll devote an entire chapter to partnership taxation matters. We do so in Chapter 7: Partnership LLC Rules.

Where there is a single-member business endeavor, the proprietorship form is automatic. No Form 8832 is required. Without the form, the proprietor is solely and personally liable for his business decisions, and for those liability actions perceived to be associated with his business activities. To achieve some protection against personal liability, the proprietor may do one of three things, namely—

    (i)   purchase a million-dollar liability insurance policy;

(ii)   register as an LLC in his state of domicile; or
(iii) register as a C or S corporation (an unlikely preference where LLC is a choice).

If a single-member business registers as an LLC, he can elect on Form 8839 to be: *disregarded as a separate entity.* This frees him from the complexity of filing corporation tax returns, and enables him to continue filing Schedules C or F (Form 1040), as appropriate. As you'll learn in Chapters 5 and 6, single member LLCs require great attention to the tax and financial isolation of business affairs.

Consent Statement & Signature(s)

The entire lower one-third portion of Form 8832 is a signature block captioned: ***Consent Statement and Signature(s).*** The "consent statement" consists of an *Under penalties of perjury* statement that those who sign below consent to the tax classification election "indicated above." The statement goes on to establish that each signatory has examined the form and finds it to be "true, correct, and complete."

There are six signatory lines columned into *Signature, Date,* and *Title.* The instructions say that if more than six signatures are involved, a *Continuation Sheet* may be used. A continuation sheet can be another copy or two (or three) of blank forms, sequentially attached and numbered. Or, it can be a separate sheet of the entity's own making, exactly duplicating the consent statement and signature block format.

For a newly-formed LLC, the unanimous consent of all owner-members is required. Each member examines the election choice, signs and dates a signature line, then enters his/her/its "title." The common title for all signers would be: "LLC member." If there were 10 required signatures, for example, each signer could affix a sequential number, such as #1 of 10; #2 of 10; #3 of 10; . . . #10 of 10. This way all members can be fully accounted for in the consent statement and signature block of Form 8832.

When changing from one elected tax classification to another on Form 8832, only a majority of owner-member signatures is required. Better yet, if the Articles of Organization filed with state authorities so provide, an officer, manager, or designated member may sign for all members of the entity. A single signature is certainly a practical arrangement where members are scattered geographically throughout the U.S. and the world. But it carries some tax risk for the nonsigners. If operations turn sour in the business, or if rampant tax abuses are perceived, those who did not sign the consent statement have to swallow hard and pay their share of the consequences. Nonsigners of any document always have difficulty recalling why or what they did not sign.

The original Form 8832, when properly executed, is filed (as a separate document of its own) with the IRS Center at Philadelphia, PA 19255. One copy is attached to the entity's first tax return or other information return for the year in which the election is to take effect. A separate copy should be furnished to and retained by each owner-member of the LLC. We depict the importance of all of this in Figure 4.2.

The 60-Month Rule

There is a bit of wisdom in requiring all LLC owner-members to consent to the Form 8832 tax classification election. Presumably, each signer, protecting his own economic interests, acts as a check and balance on the other signers to see that business and tax affairs are conducted properly. In any venture, it takes a few operational years for matters to work themselves out and settle down into an objective business stride. This is the theory on which the 60-month rule is based.

Its substance is that once a tax election is made, the entity must endure 60 months (5 years) before changing to another tax classification. The exact official wording is prescribed in IRS Regulation § 301.7701-3(c)(1)(iv): *Elections; Limitation.* The pertinent wording is—

*If an eligible entity makes an election to change its classification . . . the entity cannot change its classification by election again during the **sixty** months succeeding the effective date of the election. . . . An election by a newly formed eligible entity that is* *effective on the date of formation is not considered a change for purposes* [hereof].

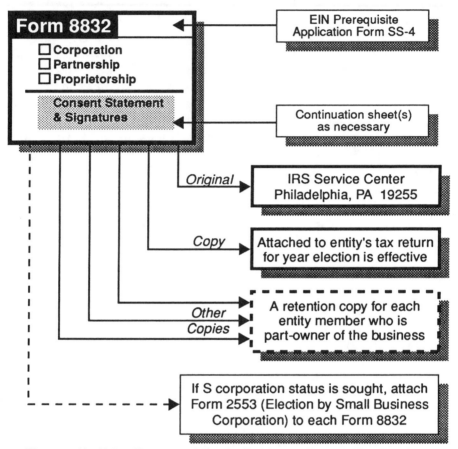

Fig. 4.2 - Notifying "Interested Parties" of Latest Income Tax Election

The idea is to avoid tax abuses by whipsaw. In any newly-formed business arrangement, members come and go. A change in membership alone is not a change in tax classification. Inevitably, though, there'll be one or more aggressive members who want to make their financial "kill" and get out. Before they get out, they persuade other members to change the tax classification to the aggressors' liking. Immediately after the effective date of change, the aggressors depart. This leaves the duped members to struggle with the tax accounting and debt reconciliation problems brought on by the change. Because of infatuation with the "limited liability" concept of an LLC, our belief is that *tax whipsawing* and *debt whipsawing* could become widespread among LLC businesses. Somebody has to pay tax on the profits. Somebody has to satisfy suppliers, creditors, and customers. Somebody has to be responsible for clear-cut derelictions of duty. Being an LLC does not convey a "free pass" by any stretch.

Incidentally, the 60-month rule does not apply if an LLC is merged with or acquired by another business entity which has a different tax classification from that of the LLC's classification.

Furthermore, the IRS may permit a classification change within 60 months—

If more than 50% of the ownership interests in the entity, as of the effective date of the subsequent election, are owned by persons that did not own any interests in the entity on the filing date . . . of the entity's prior election [as per Regulation citation above].

In way of summarizing the 60-month rule, we present Figure 4.3. The message intended there is that once an LLC is duly formed, it should stick to its initial classification until some truly bona fide business reason necessitates otherwise. This means giving the initial Form 8832 serious forethought and analysis.

Consequences of Change

There are four possible tax classification changes when using election Form 8832. The possibilities are:

1. A partnership elects to be an association, taxable as a corporation.
2. An association elects to be a partnership.
3. A solo corporation elects to be a disregarded entity, taxable as a proprietorship.
4. A disregarded entity elects to be an association, taxable as a solo corporation.

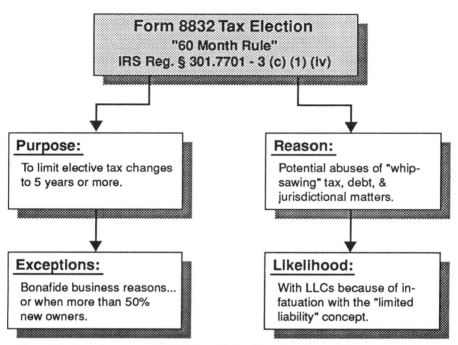

Fig. 4.3 - Key Aspects of "60-Month Rule" on Tax Classification Changes

In no case, can a partnership (of two or more members) elect to be taxable as a disregarded entity (sole proprietorship). Conversely, in no case can a disregarded entity (single member) elect to be taxable as a partnership. The reason is obvious. Any two or more owners of a business must either be a partnership (by default) or an association (by election). Any single owner business must either be a proprietorship (by default) or an association (by election.)

When there are changes in membership of two or more, there is no change to the existing tax classification: partnership or association. When a two-member entity is reduced to one member, there is a default change to a disregarded entity (proprietorship). Conversely, when a single-member activity increases to two members, there is also a default change: to a partnership.

Whether a classification change is by election or by default, there are tax and accounting consequences. Form 8832 does nothing to change the relevant provisions of the Internal Revenue Code. There is a host of provisions applicable separately to corporations, partnerships, and proprietorships. Being an LLC does not change any of the established tax laws currently in effect. For example, when an LLC partnership changes to a corporation, it has to file a termination Form 1065 (as a partnership), then start its new classification under Form 1120 rules (as a C or S corporation). Or,

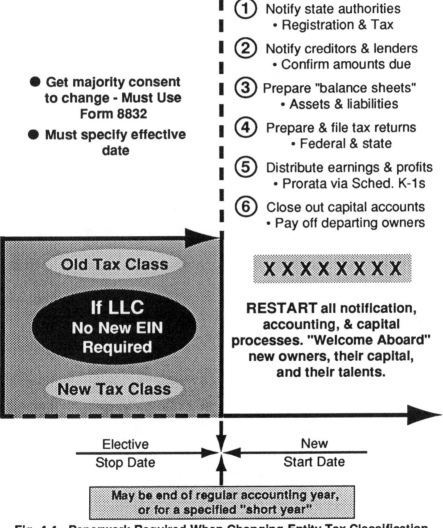

- **Get majority consent to change - Must Use Form 8832**
- **Must specify effective date**

① Notify state authorities
  • Registration & Tax

② Notify creditors & lenders
  • Confirm amounts due

③ Prepare "balance sheets"
  • Assets & liabilities

④ Prepare & file tax returns
  • Federal & state

⑤ Distribute earnings & profits
  • Prorata via Sched. K-1s

⑥ Close out capital accounts
  • Pay off departing owners

Old Tax Class

If LLC No New EIN Required

New Tax Class

X X X X X X X X

RESTART all notification, accounting, & capital processes. "Welcome Aboard" new owners, their capital, and their talents.

Elective Stop Date

New Start Date

May be end of regular accounting year, or for a specified "short year"

Fig. 4.4 - Paperwork Required When Changing Entity Tax Classification

if the LLC partnership is reduced to one member, it has to terminate the partnership, then start under Form 1040 rules: Schedule C (business) or Schedule F (farming). In each case, membership capital accounting has to be closed on one date, then restarted the next day. The same applies to the earnings and profits of the entity. As long as the entity remains an LLC, no change in EIN is required. But if the entity reregisters under state law in a business form other than an LLC, a new EIN must be obtained. The more cavalier and undisciplined the business is run, the more complicated the change consequences become. The general effect of these consequences is depicted in Figure 4.4. After studying Figure 4.4, do you now see the wisdom of the 60-month rule?

Foreign Entity "Relevance"

One ordinarily thinks of a foreign entity as being owned by nonresident aliens, who seek to do business within the U.S. When said owners do so, they come under U.S. tax laws. Said tax laws apply only when *income* is derived by a branch of the foreign entity operating in the U.S. Such income is said to be "relevant" for U.S. tax withholding purposes.

The issue of relevancy of Form 8832 to foreign entities depends on what a withholding agent in the U.S. must do. Code Sections 1441 through 1446 cover the withholding of tax on U.S. income generated by nonresident aliens (as disregarded entities), foreign partnerships, and foreign corporations. Collectively, these sections are called: *collection-at-source* rules. That is, the U.S. tax (at "rounded rates") are collected and credited to a foreign entity's U.S. tax account, before money is transferred overseas to the entity owners. All collection-at-source rules are *very* complicated. Section 1441: *Withholding of Tax on Nonresident Aliens*, for example, comprises over 1,200 statutory words and approximately 92,000 regulatory words! Relevant tax treaties, immigration rules, and international business arrangements complicate matters even further. U.S. classification is no longer relevant when a foreign entity ceases generating U.S. income for 60 consecutive months.

5

TAX FORMS & SCHEDULES

Most Federal Taxation Rules Treat An LLC As A Partnership. A Special Checkbox On Form 1065 Provides For This. Once Checked, The Term "Partner" Is Construed To Mean "LLC Member." An LLC Partnership Is NOT A Taxable Entity. Instead, All Net Income, Loss, Credits, And Certain Deductions "Pass Through" To Individual Members For Inclusion On Forms 1040. The Hallmark For Limited Liability Protection Is "Schedule L": A Balance Sheet Of Assets, Liabilities, And Capital. Such Schedule Is Absent From A Single Member LLC In Proprietorship Form. Because So, A Solo S Corporation Is Preferable For One Person LLCs.

The IRS publishes over **1,500** — yes, one thousand, five hundred (1,540 by our count) — tax forms and schedules. If you scan the Topical Index to these forms, you will not find among the "L"s a form captioned: *Limited Liability Company*. We have tipped you off to this situation in our head summary above. You have to know, or be told, that there's a checkbox on Schedule B of Form 1065 for designating the form as being for a limited liability company or LLC. [Actually, the checkbox is labeled: *Domestic* LLC, to differentiate from a Foreign LLC.] Form 1065 is titled: ***U.S. Return of Partnership Income***; its Schedule B is titled: ***Other Information***. The first item there asks: *What type of entity is filing this return? Check the applicable box.*

Form 1065 is a summary and transmittal form. It consists of four pages, included in which are six schedules: A, B, K, L, M-1, and M-2. In addition, there may be as many as 10 or so applicable schedules which are separate from, but attached to Form 1065. Furthermore, certain nonform attachments are necessary when furnishing information that is not addressed in the official forms and schedules.

We can sense your reaction now. You're probably thinking to yourself: "Is this guy going to drag me through 15 to 20 tax forms that I'm not interested in? What's the bottom line? I'm only interested in the highlights. Where do I sign? What's the tax bite? What tax writeoffs do I get? What's this partnership nonsense; what about LLCs? What if I'm a single member LLC?"

These are good questions, and we intend to address them. Before we do, though, a few preliminaries are in order. We assume, initially, that the LLC you are interested in will file Form 1065. This is a partnership return in which you associate with two or more LLC persons. If you are, or intend to be, a single member LLC, you'll understand the LLC requirements better after some familiarity with partnership LLCs. Our focus in this chapter is entirely on domestic LLCs. Foreign LLCs have to meet additional tax and state registration requirements, which we'll discuss in Chapter 12.

Regardless of the LLC entity you may participate in, the entity itself will have to file certain tax information forms with the IRS. You have no choice over this. Consequently, whatever the entity files **will affect** your own personal income tax return. Such personal return, as you know, is **Form 1040**: *U.S. Individual Income Tax Return*. You want the "bottom line": let's start with Form 1040.

Where on Form 1040?

It would be helpful if you had a Form 1040 in front of you. Look for the *Income* portion on its page 1. There are 15 lines there for entering different types of income or loss. Do you see any line caption with the term: Limited liability company or LLC? As a person interested in LLC affairs, wouldn't you expect to find some line on Form 1040 for reporting LLC income or loss? It's there indirectly . . . but you have to know where to look.

We informed you above that LLC matters are reported to the IRS on Form 1065 (for partnerships). Where on Form 1040 is there any mention of partnerships? It's there on **line 17** (year 2001 version). Said line reads—

*Rental real estate, royalties, partnerships, S corporations, trusts, etc. **Attach Schedule E.***

Schedule E (Form 1040) is titled: ***Supplemental Income and Loss***. In short, Schedule E is for the reporting of income and loss from those activities which, in general, are not your primary source of livelihood. Thus, unless you are a single member LLC participating full time therein, Schedule E is your first LLC form with which to gain familiarity.

Where on Schedule E are LLC matters reported? They go in Part II of Schedule E which is titled: ***Income or Loss from Partnerships and S Corporations***. We believe that within a few years this title will be enhanced to include LLCs. In the meantime, you have to mentally associate your LLC activities with partnerships.

Part II is at the top of page 2 of Schedule E (Form 1040). Where and what do you have to report? To aid you in this regard, we present in Figure 5.1 highlights of the candidate applicable items that address an LLC. We have indicated a bottom line there, which is not the bottom line of the entire Schedule E form. We are assuming that your only supplemental activity is an LLC. On this basis, you can see that the bottom line of Part II is a combination of information from checkboxes, columns, line entries, and other separate forms which you may have to attach to your Form 1040.

Note in Figure 5.1 that there are three forms, one section, and one schedule mentioned. We have indicated these in bold print. While not indicated on the official Part II, the titles of these forms are:

Sec. 179   — Election to Expense Certain Depreciable Business Assets

Form 4562   — Depreciation and Amortization

Form 6198   — At-Risk Limitations

Part III Sch.E (1040)	Income or Loss From Partnerships, S Corporations, [and LLCs]			Year	
	If at-risk activity : Form 6198			**At Risk?**	
Name of Entity		Type	Tax I.D.	All	Some
A					
B					
C					

PASSIVE Income/Loss		**NONPASSIVE Income/Loss**			
Loss From Form 8582	Income From Schedule K-1	Loss From Schedule K-1	Sec. 179 Exp. Form 4562	Income From Schedule K-1	
A					
B					
C					

	Add all income amounts	
	Add all loss & Sec. 179 amounts	< >
	● Combine & enter result on page 1, Form 1040	

Fig. 5.1 - Part II, Sch. E (Form 1040) Abbreviated for Instructional Purposes

Form 8582   — Passive Activity Loss Limitations

Schedule K-1 — Partner's Share of Income, Credits, Deductions, etc. [Read "Partner's" as "LLC Member's" share . . .]

Also note in Figure 5.1 that there are two major columnar spacings. One column (consisting of two subcolumns) is captioned: *Passive Income and Loss.* The other column (consisting of three subcolumns) is captioned: *Nonpassive Income and Loss.* Do you know the difference? Your LLC may have elements of both. Do you know what Forms 4562, 6198, and 8582 are all about? Your LLC reportings may involve any one or all three of these forms.

Are you beginning to get the message that we want you to get?

The message is: There is no quick-fix, one figure, bottom-line amount that you can pluck out of the LLC air and enter it on Form 1040 as your share of the LLC's net income or net loss.

With the exception of Schedule K-1 (Form 1065), most of the other terms and forms that we show in Figure 5.1 are covered, or at least mentioned in Chapters 7 through 11 herein. We have yet to address your bottom line concerns with respect to Schedule K-1.

Schedule K-1: Top 1/3

As already cited, the title of Schedule K-1 (Form 1065) is: *Partner's* [Singular] *Share of Income, Credits, Deductions, etc.* This is a 2-page form: front and back. Below the title on page 1 there are two address blocks. These are—

Partner's identifying number [left-hand side]
Partnership's identifying number [right-hand side]

Right off, this information conveys that if there are 10 LLC members in the partnership, 10 Schedules K-1 must be prepared. The original of each K-1 goes directly to the IRS, as an attachment to Form 1065. You get a photocopy of the original with your name, address, and Tax I.D. on it. You transfer designated entry amounts to your own return, then keep the K-1 for your records.

Below the two address blocks, there is a portion which we call: "Information and capital account." The address blocks and the information portion take up about 1/3 of Page 1 of Schedule K-1. The information portion consists of 10 items: "A" through "J". Your capital account portion consists of five columned entry blocks. So important is this information to you as an LLC member that we present it all (abbreviated where necessary) in Figure 5.2. We urge you to take a moment and read through all the words in this figure.

Item A, though abbreviated in Figure 5.2, reads in full as—

This partner is a ☐ *general partner* ☐ *limited partner* ☐ *limited liability company member.*

When the LLC box is checked, it is your cue that wherever the words "partner" or "partnership" appear, you substitute "LLC member" or "LLC entity," respectively.

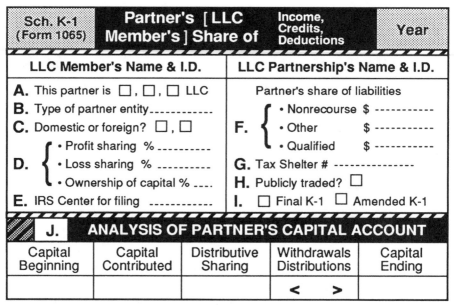

Fig. 5.2 - Top 1/3 of Schedule K-1 (Form 1065) Abbreviated

Item B tells you that an LLC member may be other than an individual: it may be an entity (another LLC, a partnership, corporation, or trust). Item C clarifies whether your LLC is domestic or foreign. Items E, G, H, and I are self-explanatory in Figure 5.2.

Item D is your profit/loss sharing and ownership percentages. Item F is your share of LLC liabilities. Item J is a recap of your capital account activities for the reported tax year. The entries at all three of these items should be verified from your own records as based on terms of the LLC's Operating Agreement. Said agreement is part of the LLC's required records. You were supposed to have been given an opportunity to participate in, read, and sign that agreement. Whether you were or not, we urge you to get a copy of that agreement and keep it with your capital accounting records. We devote considerable attention to capital accounting in Chapter 7: Partnership LLC Rules.

Items D, F, and J do not represent any bottom-line income or loss. They comprise what is reported to the IRS as your capital interests in the LLC arrangement. They also define your exposure to liability, should a successful lawsuit be brought against the LLC. If you are derelict in maintaining your agreed share of the LLC's capital base, or, worse, if you engage in wrongful conduct in any way, you expose yourself to personal liability in excess of your capital account with the LLC. Thus, that which appears in the top 1/3 portion of your Schedule K-1 should be taken seriously. None of this information goes on Schedule E (Form 1040).

Distributive Share Items

By far, the primary use of Schedule K-1 is its distributive share information which goes on various forms and schedules that attach to Form 1040. For this purpose, there are **56** entry lines on Schedule K-1. Of this number, 25 lines are on page 1; 27 lines are on page 2. All 56 lines are grouped into the following eight categories:

- Income (Loss)
- Deductions
- Credits
- Investment Interest
- Self-Employment
- Adjustments & Tax Preferences
- Foreign Taxes
- Other

An overview of the categorization and columnarization of these 56 lines is presented in Figure 5.3. Obviously, we've done a lot of abbreviation in our depiction.

Of the three columns in Figure 5.3, **Column (c)** is where we want to focus at this moment. In Column (c) you are directed, where applicable, to as many as five Form 1040 schedules (A, B, D, E, and SE) and to 10 or so other forms which may have to be attached to Form 1040. To know which form or schedule you need, you are told in numerous places in Column (c):

See page _____ of Partner's Instructions for Schedule K-1 (Form 1065)

Continuation of Fig. 5.2		
(a) Distributive Share Item	**(b) Amount**	**1040 Filers (C) Enter Col.(b) on**
Income (Loss) **13 lines**	$	See Text & Official Instructions
Deductions **4 lines**	"	"
Credits **8 lines**	"	"
Investment Interest **3 lines**	"	"
Self-Employment **3 lines**	"	"
Adjustments & Preferences **6 lines**	"	"
Foreign Taxes **11 lines**	"	"
Other **8 lines**	"	"
Supplemental Information		

Fig. 5.3 - General Format of Distributive Share Items on Schedule K-1

These "partner's instructions" cover 10+ pages of official text . . . or about 15,000 words.

The only information that goes directly onto Schedule E (1040) from Schedule K-1 (1065) is the following lines:

line 1 — Ordinary income (loss) from trade or business activities

line 2 — Net income (loss) from rental real estate activities

line 3 — Net income (loss) from other rental activities

line 4c — Royalties

line 9 — Section 179 expense deduction

Even these lines require referencing the partner's Schedule K-1 instructions.

The very last line on page 2 of Schedule K-1 is identified as line 25. Actually, this is the 57th line, because many lines have sublines: a, b, c, etc. Nevertheless, line 25 consists of six full-width blank lines (shown in Figure 5.3 as *Supplemental Information*). The caption there reads—

> *Supplemental information required to be reported separately to each partner (attach additional schedules if more space is needed):*

This blank-line space is useful when a member materially participates in an LLC activity; when he lends money to, or borrows money from, the LLC; or when his distributive share is based on less than 365 days of the taxable year.

All in all, Schedule K-1 is a formidable tax "information" document. As an LLC member, it is issued to you without any action on your part. It is **not** a tax return. It is information you need when preparing your own return. Unless you familiarize yourself with it, preferably with the aid of the 10+ pages of IRS instructions, you may miss the tax benefits that pass on to you.

The Origin of Schedule K-1

Unless a member is expressly so designated in the LLC operating agreement, the Schedule K-1 is not prepared by member recipients. The preparation is done under the accounting auspices of the Tax Matters Member. The K-1 itself does not evolve until after Form 1065: U.S. Return of Partnership Income, is completed. This is a 4-page form of which page 3 constitutes the origin of the information that goes on Schedule K-1. The full length of page 3 is Schedule K: *Partners' Shares of Income, Credits, Deductions, etc.* Note with special care that Schedule K is **plural**: Partners' Shares of . . ., whereas Schedule K-1 is *singular*: Partner's Share of . . . . The placement of the apostrophe (s' or 's) makes a world of difference. In the aggregate, there is an amount called: "partners' capital," which, generally, is the target for lawsuits.

Schedule K (the one with the s') summarizes the membership pass-through tax items that derive from all books, records, and activities of the LLC entity for the year. The line numbers and line captions on Schedule K correspond identically with those on Schedule K-1 (the one with the 's). In this manner, whatever entry amount is on a line on Schedule K appears, with modification, on its corresponding line on Schedule K-1. The "modification" is *each member's percentage* of profit sharing, loss sharing, and ownership of capital (as appropriate).

For example, if a line entry on Schedule K showed $1,286 and a particular member's percentage interest was 17.76%, the amount transferred to Schedule K-1 would be—

$1,286 x 0.1776 = $228 (rounded).

Imagine having 10 LLC members, each with a different percentage of sharing, and a Schedule K with eight entry amounts on it. This would require the preparation of 10 Schedules K-1. Each such K-1 would have eight different entries of fractioned amounts from Schedule K. That would be 80 separate computations to be made. The accompanying accounting tasks require extraordinary backup worksheets to placate any skeptical K-1 recipient. Unless all LLC members familiarize themselves with the K-1 process (as we urge above), one recalcitrant recipient — he who demands a single, simple, bottom-line amount — could cause the other nine members to be late in receiving their K-1s. Any K-1 lateness, in turn, causes each recipient to be late when filing his own individual Form 1040.

The Allure of Form 1065

As recently mentioned, Form 1065 (the partnership return) consists of four pages. We've already described one of these pages: page 3 — Schedule K. The 1065 additionally includes the attachment of designated forms, schedules, and statements where applicable.

The first item noteworthy at this point is the last full line in the head block to page 1 of Form 1065. It reads—

Number of Schedules K-1. Attach one for each person who was a partner [LLC member] *at any time during the tax year* ▶ _____

This item closes the loop on an earlier statement we made about the originals of each K-1 being attached to Form 1065.

Neither Schedule K nor any of the Schedules K-1 is signed by anyone. Being part of Form 1065, they are authenticated by the signature(s) appearing at the bottom of its page 1. The principal signature is that of the general partner or of an LLC member. If the return is prepared professionally, the preparer's signature also appears. Both signatures follow a jurat clause: *Under penalties of perjury . . . that Form 1065 . . . including accompanying schedules and statements . . . is true, correct, and complete.*

Otherwise, the bulk of page 1 is a straightforward profit and loss statement. A preprinted **Caution** states: *Include only trade or business income and expenses.* Some 22 lines and four sublines are preprinted for this purpose. There is an **Income** portion, with line 8 captioned: ***Total income (loss).*** There is a **Deductions** portion, with line 21 captioned: ***Total deductions.*** Line 22 is the "bottom line" (of page 1 only). Its full caption is—

Ordinary income (loss) from trade or business activities.

Believe this or not: The line 22, page 1, is the **only information** transferred from Form 1065 to Schedule K. It goes onto line 1 of Schedule K. The caption for that line of Schedule K is identical to that above. This is followed by the parenthetical notation (from *page 1, line 22* of Form 1065).

There is a line 2 and some 50 other lines on Schedule K. Where does their information come from? It comes from other forms and schedules that attach to Schedule K. For example, line 2 on Schedule K reads—

Net income (loss) from rental real estate activities. (Attach Form 8825).

Form 8825: What's that? Its title is: ***Rental Real Estate Income and Expenses of a Partnership*** [LLC] ***or an S corporation.***

Other lines on Schedule K (not all) carry preprinted instructions to attach specific forms or schedules. Those lines absent preprinted instructions derive their information from the *Specific Instructions to Schedule K* (some 12 pages of text).

Here, now, we have revealed the tax mechanics of a little-known fact. Because, by design, Schedule K is automatically part of Form 1065, it accommodates any number of different activities engaged in by a partnership or LLC. There is no statutory limit. The allure of such flexibility is truly fascinating. The only entrepreneurial limitations are management skills and the financial base for operations.

The Balance Sheets

No other tax document describes the financial health of an LLC better than its balance sheets. There is a balance sheet for the beginning of the year and, separately, one for the end of the year. Differences between the balance sheets from one year to the next represent either growth, stagnation, or decline of the enterprise. A balance sheet, as you know, is a statement of the assets, liabilities, and capital of an entity. Such information is not part of Schedule K or Schedule K-1.

There is a separate schedule of its own for listing the assets and liabilities of an LLC. It is **Schedule L**: *Balance Sheets per Books*. This schedule takes up half of page 4 of Form 1065. The instructions for Schedule L say—

The balance sheets should agree with the [LLC's] *books and records. Attach a statement explaining any differences.*

We present in Figure 5.4 an abridged (and slightly edited) replica of Schedule L (Form 1065). We say "abridged" because we show only two of the four official columns. We urge that you take a moment and read down each of the 26 line items there. Such reading alone is instructive in that it gives you a feel for why we believe Schedule L is so important.

Technically, if total receipts are less than $250,000 **and** total assets (at end of year) are less than $600,000, no Schedule L is IRS

SCHEDULE L	BALANCE SHEETS	• Beginning of Year [Cols. (a) & (b)] • End of Year [Cols. (c) & (d)]		
		ASSETS	(c)	(d)
1	Cash		///	
2a	Accounts receivable			///
b	**LESS** allowances for bad debts			
3	Inventories		///	
4	U.S. Government obligations		///	
5	Tax-exempt securities		///	
6	Other current assets		///	
7	Mortgage & real estate loans		///	
8	Other investments		///	
9a	Buildings & other depreciable assets			///
b	**LESS** accumulated depreciation			
10a	Depletable assets			///
b	**LESS** accumulated depreciation			
11	Land		///	
12a	Intangible assets			///
b	**LESS** accumulated amortization			
13	Other assets		///	
14	**Total Assets** ///////////////		///	
	LIABILITIES & CAPITAL		///	///
15	Accounts payable		///	
16	Mortgages, notes payable < 1 year		///	
17	Other current liabilities		///	
18	**ALL nonrecourse loans**		///	
19	Mortgages, notes payable > 1 year		///	
20	Other liabilities		///	
21	**Partners' capital accounts**		///	
22	**Total Liabilities & Capital** ///////////		///	
	Attach explanations			

Fig. 5.4 - Edited/Abbreviated End-of-Year LLC Balance Sheet

required. It takes a lot of work to get the balance sheets in balance. Not doing so, even when not required, inevitably raises suspicions about the accounting discipline, management efficiency, and financial health of the LLC. Without the balance sheets, members tend to argue among themselves, creditors worry about being paid, and plaintiffs' attorneys see an opening for the kill. Having no balance sheets tends to destroy the legitimacy of a protective shield against the personal liability of LLC members. As you'll see below, a balance sheet intertwines with members' capital accounts.

On the liabilities side of the balancing effort, there is one item that requires close attention and control. It is item 18 (in Figure 5.4): *All nonrecourse loans*. A nonrecourse loan is a liability of the entity for which no LLC member bears the economic risk of loss. Lacking this member risk, there is temptation to wheel and deal at the entity level without serious concentration on growing the business and its net worth. Because total liabilities and capital must equal total assets, it should be self-evident that the greater the amount of nonrecourse loans, the less the partners' [LLC members'] capital accounts. Low capital accounts imply a cavalier attitude towards the entire LLC operation.

Capital Accounts Reconciliation

On Schedule L, there is no direct, stand-alone entry item for the impact of net income or loss from an LLC's year-long operation. It appears indirectly in the members' capital accounts. The "indirection" is several reconciliation steps between Schedules K and L. For starters, there is a subschedule insert just above Schedule L which is captioned: *Analysis of Net Income (Loss)*. By following the preprinted instructions thereon, an *aggregate* net income or loss is established.

Below Schedule L, there is a Schedule M-2 titled: *Analysis of Partners' Capital Accounts*. Schedule M-2 plays the pivotal role in the whole reconciliation and balancing process. A depiction of such is presented in Figure 5.5. As you can sense, there is a delicate interlock between the LLC members' *aggregate* capital accounts (Schedule M-2) and the individual accounts displayed on Schedules K-1, all of which in turn appear as one combined item (line 21) on

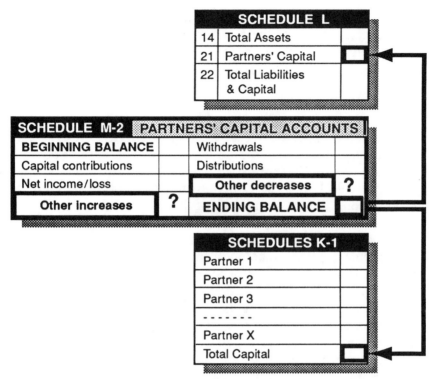

Fig. 5.5 - The Pivotal Balancing Role of Schedule M-2

Schedule L. To achieve the perfect interlock, a lot of trial and error juggling goes on. The instructions to Schedule M-2 say—

> *The amounts of Schedule M-2 should equal the total of the amounts reported in **item J** of all the partners'* [LLC members'] *Schedules K-1. . . . If the capital balances differ from the amounts reported on Schedule L, attach a statement reconciling any differences.*

Item J on Schedule K-1 is a near-replica of Schedule M-2 for each LLC member, separately.

Perhaps, now, you realize why Schedule L: *Balance Sheets per Books*, is so important to the tax and legal credibility of an LLC. Having no such schedule, or having one that is incomplete (re Schedule M-1: *Reconciliation of Income (Loss) per Books with*

Income (Loss) per Return and Schedule M-2), raises questions about the correctness of the K-1s. Any absence or incompleteness on page 4 of Form 1065 (where Schedule L is) is a natural magnet for personal liability lawsuits.

Single Member LLCs

As indicated previously, single member LLCs are recognized under various state laws. A solo LLC, however, cannot operate in partnership form. There must be two or more LLC members to do so. Thus, a solo LLC has to operate either as a proprietorship or as a corporation. Let us address each of these two options separately.

As a proprietorship, whether an LLC or an ordinary proprietorship, there is no distinction in federal tax forms and schedules that applies. Where a form or schedule calls for the entry of a name, the LLC proprietor simply follows his business name with the letters: LLC. A fictitious business name should be used. This is to more clearly distinguish the business from the proprietor's personal name. For example, "Ducks-in-a-Row, LLC" sounds more like a business activity than does "John J. Jones, LLC" who is the sole proprietor of Ducks-in-a-Row.

There is a significant legal difference between an LLC proprietorship and an ordinary proprietorship. An LLC proprietorship has to go through the same state-forming formalities as a partnership LLC. We covered such matters in Chapter 2: Forming an LLC. In contrast, an ordinary proprietorship need only file a *Fictitious Business Name Statement* with the County Clerk's Office, in the county where the proprietor does business. As a result, an ordinary proprietorship can claim no LL (limited liability) protection whatsoever.

To claim the LL protection, an LLC proprietorship is looked upon as a lesser form of LLC partnership. Taxwise, any trade or business income or loss are reported on similar forms: Schedule C (Form 1040) versus page 1 of Form 1065. The entry line captions, including those for cost of goods sold, are nearly identical. The Schedule C is titled: *Profit or Loss from Business*. There is also a Schedule F (Form 1040) titled: *Profit or Loss from Farming*. Interestingly, one of the income items on page 1 of Form 1065 is—

Net farm profit (loss) (attach Schedule F (Form 1040)).

If an LLC proprietor wants to engage in one or more rental real estate activities, he can do so. He can be the sole owner of such property or properties. He can be a joint owner with his spouse or a co-owner with other individuals. As a proprietorship, however, Part I of Schedule E (Form 1040) is used in lieu of Part II for a partnership. Part I is titled: ***Income or Loss from Rental Real Estate and Royalties***. Otherwise, Parts I and II treat all tax matters equivalently.

With respect to portfolio activities (stocks, bonds, etc.) and the acquisition and sale of business property, there are no tax form distinctions between a proprietorship LLC and a partnership LLC.

Where the truly major difference exists is the matter of balance sheets: assets, liabilities, and capital. For a proprietorship LLC, there is no counterpart to the Schedule L: ***Balance Sheet per Books*** of a partnership LLC. Proprietorships, whether LLC or otherwise, are simply not tax-required to post balance sheets each year. Should a proprietorship LLC become the target of a lawsuit, the owner would have to scramble to put together a Schedule L-like statement. Pulling together such a statement from among commingled personal and business records does not bode well for the "defining moment" of LL protection.

Solo S Corporation

If an LLC proprietor is seriously concerned about his exposure to personal liability lawsuits, a solo S corporation is the better option to pursue. This is assuming that the business is being conducted in a responsible and prudent way. To pursue this option, check the box at line 2a of Form 8832: ***Entity Classification Election*** that reads—

☐ *A domestic eligible entity electing to be classed as an association taxable as a corporation.*

There are two basic types of corporations: C and S. The C corporation is taxable on its net earnings and profits *before* any dividends are paid to shareholders. An S corporation, by comparison, is not taxed at the corporate level. Instead, the earnings and profits are passed through to shareholders who are then taxed. In this "pass-through" aspect, an S corporation and a partnership are identical. There are some taxation exceptions (for built-in carryovers) where an S corporation is formed by conversion from a predecessor C corporation. Our focus is the S corporation for which there is no C corporation predecessor.

For a solo S corporation, IRS Form 1120S is required. This form is titled: **U.S. *Income Tax Return for an S Corporation*.** Like the partnership Form 1065, Form 1120S also has four pages. Pages 1 and 2, where directed at: *Ordinary income (loss) from trade or business activities*, are very similar on Forms 1065 and 1120S. Page 3 of both forms consists of Schedule K. Page 4 of both forms consists of Schedules L, M-1, and M-2. Except for terminology and adjustments for partners' capital accounts and shareholders' equity accounts, there are no functional differences between Schedules K, L, and M whether a partnership or an S corporation. Whatever limited liability protection is afforded a partnership by virtue of its Schedule L (Balance Sheets per Books) is afforded equally to a solo S corporation. We cannot say this for a proprietorship LLC.

There is one more reason for preferring a solo S corporation to a proprietorship LLC. If the business prospers, and you want additional capital for growth, you can always add one, two, or more LLC member shareholders to the company roster. You'll only need to amend the single member LLC operating agreement. Otherwise, there are no federal tax forms and schedules to change. Best of all: You do not have to resell yourself as an LLC entity.

6

CALIFORNIA FORM 568

California Has Its Own "Return Of Income" Tax Form For LLCs Doing Business Within Its Borders, Whether Organized In State Or Out of State. The Reason: California Imposes An LLC Tax, An LLC Franchise Fee, And Withholds Income Tax On Nonconsenting NONRESIDENT Members. Integral With Its Form Are Schedules K And K-1 For Distributive Share Items. These Schedules Start With Federal Amounts, Adjust For California Differences, And Apply An APPORTIONMENT FORMULA To Arrive At California SOURCE Amounts From A Mixture Of Multi-State Income. The California Form Is Highly Instructive.

General partnerships and ordinary proprietorships require no "licensing" by the Secretary of State where the business is organized and conducted. Each such entity can start a profit-seeking activity in good faith, abide by the general business code of the state . . . and that's it. There is no periodic certification, filing, or licensing fee involved. Why so?

Simple answer. There is no limited liability protection to general partners and sole proprietors. The owners of these forms of business are personally liable for wrongful acts, regardless of whatever capital base they maintain.

When it comes to an LLC entity, whether a partnership LLC or a proprietorship LLC, all states impose a "fee" of some kind. The fee is for the filing, certification, and updating of the Articles of Organization and the LLC's List of Managers. Beyond this, income tax matters are handled by a separate agency of the state. Not all states, however, impose income taxes. There are nine states that do not. (We'll list these nine states later.)

California takes the fee and tax business to a new level. In addition to the Secretary of State's fee, California's Franchise Tax Board imposes an LLC fee AND an LLC tax. This fee and tax is **in addition to** the income tax imposed on LLC members individually. Furthermore, the LLC fee and LLC tax apply equally to partnership LLCs and proprietorship LLCs. All of which justifies, in California, a quite different tax form for LLCs. This is Form 568: *Limited Liability Company Return of Income*.

Accordingly, in this chapter, we want to acquaint you with the most significant features of California Form 568, and how it applies to both partnership LLCs and proprietorship LLCs. Also, we want to acquaint you with how Form 568 applies to both resident and nonresident members, whether individual or entity. We think the California form is instructive, if for no other reason than to compare it with the state in which you do business as an LLC. We think it is also instructive to see how California treats LLCs differently from the way the IRS treats LLCs.

In taxation matters, California considers itself to be an independent sovereign nation. In terms of GDP size (Gross Domestic Product), California ranks 5th in the world. As such, it imposes stringent apportionment rules between in-state and out-state sources of income. The source apportionment rules apply regardless of whether an LLC is organized in California or outside of California doing business in California.

California's "Tax on Tax"

As pointed out in the previous chapter, there is no federal income tax imposed on a partnership at the entity level. This is so, regardless of the type of partnership: general, limited, or LLC. The reason for this "no entity tax" is that all net income (loss), credits, certain deductions, etc. are passed through to entity members who are individually income taxed. This same pass-through principle applies to single-member LLCs who opt (for capital disclosure reasons) to be a solo S corporation.

Now, comes California. It treats an LLC for franchise purposes just like it treats a corporation. It imposes both a franchise tax **and** a franchise fee for the privilege of doing business in California. Neither of these two franchise impositions is regarded as an income tax, though they are based on income in the general sense. The LLC franchise tax is a flat $800 each year. It applies whether the LLC generates profit or not, or whether it generates any income at all. This is for starters.

California also imposes an LLC franchise fee based on total income for the year. For fee purposes, the term *total income* is based on the grand total **positive** income (**before** cost of goods, expenses, allowances) generated by the LLC in California. No losses whatsoever are taken into account. For example, on the matter of capital gains and losses involving business property, the Form 568 instructions say—

a. *Enter the capital gains (**not losses**) of disregarded entities* [single member LLCs in proprietorship form].

b. *Enter LLC's distributive share of capital gains (**not losses**) from pass-through entities* [partnerships, S corporations, trusts].

c. *Enter the capital gains (**not losses**) included on Schedule D (568)* [Capital Gain or Loss]

California has a 36-line worksheet for computing an LLC's total income. The above example is just three lines of the 36. By not considering any otherwise allowable offsets against total income, there is no computed taxable income. Consequently, the rationale is that any amount imposed on total income is not a tax: it is a franchise fee. It is a license for the sole privilege of doing business in California. As fee rates go, it is not onerous: about 2/10ths of 1 percent (0.2%). There is no LLC fee for total incomes of less than $250,000. For total incomes between $250,000 and $5,000,000, the LLC fee ranges from $1,000 to $6,000. For total incomes over $5,000,000, the LLC fee is $9,000+. In our mind, this is another tax on income. There's still more.

If a California LLC has nonresident members — either out-of-state or out-of-country — the entity must withhold California income taxes from each such member's distributive share. The year 2000 withholding rates, for example, were 1.5% for S corporations, 8.8% for C corporations, and 9.3% for individuals, partnerships, LLCs, and fiduciaries. If a nonresident member consents in writing to California's jurisdiction over his distributive share, and promises to file a California nonresident income tax return, no withholding by the LLC entity is required.

Altogether, an LLC in California has the following financial burdens beyond those required on a federal LLC return:

LLC franchise tax	$800 annually
LLC franchise fee	0.2% of total income (approximately)
Nonresident withholdings	9+% of each member's distributive share

We don't know about you, but this appears to us like a "tax on tax." There is still income tax at each individual member's level to be addressed by California.

Overview of Form 568

We are quite aware that California's Form 568 may not be of direct interest to those readers who are LLC participants in states other than California. Nevertheless, we think that a quick skim-through will cause you to appreciate better your blessings. At the same time, you'll be on notice that a non-California LLC doing business in California will be subject to a nonresident tax imposed by California.

California's Form 568: *Limited Liability Company Return of Income*, consists of four pages. Additionally, there are numerous attachments (forms and schedules) where applicable. Its page 1 consists of the following categories:

1. Head portion — name, address, type of activity, etc.
2. Information portion — 15 Yes/No checkboxes

3. LLC tax and fee summary
4. Single member consent portion
5. Signature portion — officer or member, and preparer

We'll come back to the most significant features of page 1, shortly. Page 2 of Form 568 consists of the following schedules:

A — *Cost of Goods Sold*
B — *Income and Deductions*
T — *Nonconsenting Nonresident Members' Tax Liability*

Schedules A and B are not significantly different from similar schedules for proprietorships, partnerships, or corporations. These schedules address an ordinary trade or business, where one or more LLC members actively participate. Schedule T consists of four columns: (1) Member's name, (2) Member's federal Tax I.D., (3) Distributive share of income x tax rate, and (4) Member's tax due. Schedule T cannot be prepared until all distributed sharing has been prorata fractioned.

The entire page 3 of Form 568 is Schedule K: *Members'* [plural] *Shares of Income, Deductions, Credits, Etc.* With the exception of self-employment tax and foreign taxes (which do not apply in California), this schedule is near-identical to the federal Schedule K(1065). However, whereas the K(1065) involves two columnar amounts, the K(568) requires three columnar amounts:

Col. (a) — Amounts from federal K(1065)
Col. (b) — California adjustments
Col. (c) — Total amounts using California law

Page 4 of Form 568 consists of the following schedules:

L — *Balance Sheets*
    • Assets • Liabilities • Capital
M-1 — *Reconciliation of Income per Books*
    With Income per Return
M-2 — *Analysis of Members' Capital Accounts*
O — *Amounts from Liquidation Used to Capitalize a Limited Liability Company*

Schedules L, M-1, an M-2 are line-for-line identical with these corresponding schedules on federal Form 1065 (partnership). Instructions caution: *Use California amounts.* The preprinted instructions at Schedule O are self-explanatory. What California is looking for here are any predecessor businesses that were liquidated to form the LLC, and whether the liquidation gains (if any) were tax recognized in California . . . or elsewhere. Federal as well as California want to be apprised of potential abusive tax practices when "switching businesses around."

Page 1, Form 568 Revisited

The head portion of California Form 568 for LLCs requires virtually the same descriptive information as does federal Form 1065 for partnerships. Such information includes: Principal business activity; principal product or service; date business started; total assets at end of year; method of accounting: cash, accrual, or other. Additionally, there is a space entry (top, upper right) for: *Secretary of State file number.* This, of course, is for the coordination of administrative and legal matters between the Secretary of State and the California Franchise Tax Board.

Of the general information block, the first box space there is item J. It reads—

> *Enter the maximum number of members in the LLC at any time during the year. Attach a California Schedule K-1(568) for each of these members.* □

At this point, you become aware that there is a California Schedule K-1: *Member's* [singular] *Share of Income, Deductions, Credits, etc.* It is quite similar to the federal K-1. In the California K-1, in addition to the distributive share column (a), there are columns—

(b)   *Amounts from federal K-1(1065)*
(c)   *California adjustments*
(d)   *Total amounts using California law*
(e)   *California source amounts* [when col. (d) includes amounts from non-California sources]

Of the 15 Yes/No checkboxes following item J, most are reasonably self-explanatory. There are a few information stoppers, however. For example, item L asks—

*Is this LLC apportioning income to California using Schedule R? [**Apportionment and Allocation of Income**]* ☐ *Yes* ☐ *No*

We'll come back to Schedule R, below. The main body of page 1 of Form 568 — and probably its real reason for existence — is its LLC tax and fee portion. This portion is so significant that we replicate it (abbreviated where necessary) in Figure 6.1. This portion of the page is bold print captioned:

Attach check or money order here.

This subcaption alone tells you why California wants a totally separate LLC tax return of its own.

Single Member LLCs

Whereas we have referred federally to single member LLCs as either an LLC proprietorship or a solo S corporation, California refers to them as **SMLLCs** or disregarded entities (the "SM" is single member). The first indication of separate treatment of SMLLCs on Form 568 is item U. This two-part question reads—

U(1) *Is this LLC a business entity disregarded for tax purposes?* ☐ *Yes* ☐ *No*

U(2) *If yes, see instructions and complete Page 1 and Page 3 only. Are there credits or credit carryovers attributable to the disregarded entity?* ☐ *Yes* ☐ *No*

The "see instructions" refers to federal Form 8832: Entity Classification Election (recall Chapter 4) by requiring that a copy of it be attached to California Form 568.

Several inches below item U(2), there is a SMLLC portion which reads:

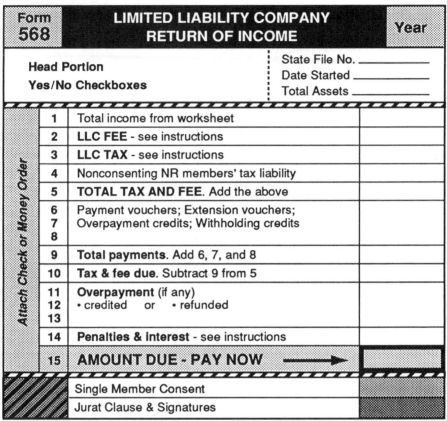

Form 568	LIMITED LIABILITY COMPANY RETURN OF INCOME		Year
Head Portion **Yes/No Checkboxes**		State File No. _____ Date Started _____ Total Assets _____	

	1	Total income from worksheet	
	2	**LLC FEE** - see instructions	
	3	**LLC TAX** - see instructions	
	4	Nonconsenting NR members' tax liability	
	5	**TOTAL TAX AND FEE.** Add the above	
	6 7 8	Payment vouchers; Extension vouchers; Overpayment credits; Withholding credits	
	9	**Total payments.** Add 6, 7, and 8	
	10	**Tax & fee due.** Subtract 9 from 5	
	11 12 13	**Overpayment** (if any) • credited or • refunded	
	14	**Penalties & interest** - see instructions	
	15	**AMOUNT DUE - PAY NOW** ⟶	

(left margin: Attach Check or Money Order)

| Single Member Consent |
| Jurat Clause & Signatures |

Fig. 6.1 - LLC Levies for Privilege of Doing Business in California

Single Member LLC Information and Consent
— Complete only if the LLC is disregarded.

The instruction here means that, if the SMLLC has opted for a solo S corporation (federal Form 1120S), the consent statement is not required. Otherwise, the SMLLC cites his company's name, federal Tax I.D., Secretary of State file number, then signs (on page 1) the following consent statement:

I consent to the jurisdiction of the State of California to tax my LLC income and agree to file returns and pay tax as may be required by the Franchise Tax Board.

The most likely California returns for a SMLLC would be—

Form 540 — *California Resident Income Tax Return*
Form 540NR — *California Nonresident or Part-Year Resident Income Tax Return*
. . . and, of course, Form 568: pages 1 and 3.

Page 3, recall, is Schedule K: distributive share items. In a SMLLC, there is no distributive sharing. All 100% of each item on Schedule K(568) goes to the sole owner. This means that for Column (b): *Amounts from federal K(1065)*, one strikes out those words and prints above them: **SMLLC**. He then goes through all of the federal forms he has filed, and enters onto the K(568) all of the matching items he can find.

Analysis: Schedule K (568)

For multi-member LLCs, Schedule K(568) is the driving force for the reconciliation efforts of Schedule M-1: *Income per Books with Income per Return*. The California instructions to Schedule K(568) say—

See federal instructions for Schedule K: Analysis of Net Income (Loss) . . . [for arriving at] *Total distributive income payment items* [the "bottom line"].

Whereas Schedule K(568) has some 40 or so possible entry amounts, by following the preprinted *Combine . . . subtract* instructions in its analysis portion, one summary amount is posted. There are 7+ "combine" lines and 6+ "subtract" lines. Each is expressly identified in the *Analysis* portion of K(568). With the exception of long-term capital gain and credit for foreign taxes paid (which California does not recognize), the "combine and subtract" lines are identical for the K(1065) and K(568). With one total distributive amount, the analysis of members begins.

We do our best in Figure 6.2 to schematize what is taking place at the "bottom line" of Schedule K. Credits and carryovers are not included. They are addressed on separate tax forms of their own.

Sched. K (568) : Members' Shares of Distributive Items			
Listed Items	Federal Amounts	California Adjustments	California Amounts
			●
			●
● COMBINE designated items			●
□ SUBTRACT designated items			□
			□

Total Distributive Income/Payments Items				- - - - - - ▶		$ Net Total Amount	
$ Amount to each member class	Individual		Corpor-ation	Partner-ship	LLC	Other	
	Active	Passive					
Near-identical to Items on federal Schedule K (1065)							

Fig. 6.2 - Analysis Taking Place at Bottom of Schedule K (568)

The "analysis" of Schedule K is the apportionment of the total distributive amount to each type of member: individual, corporation, partnership, LLC, trust, etc. The analysis does not address the number of members; we get this from the number of Schedules K-1 attached. The analysis addresses the type of member: individual or entity, and the distributive dollar amount to each class type. If there are more individual than entity members, it implies greater profit-seeking devotion.

Where a member is an individual, he must be classified as "active" or "passive." This is because passive members are subject to special loss limitation rules, which active/nonpassive members are not. For this classification effort, the federal instructions to K(1065) — which California follows — say, in paraphrased terms:

An LLC should classify each member as "active or passive" to the best of its knowledge and belief. In most cases, the level of participation in an activity will be apparent. If not apparent or readily determinable, classify the member as "passive."

Nonresident Members: List of

California is like most other income taxing states. It is very sensitive about nonresidents earning money from California sources. One can appreciate this sensitivity when being informed that the bulk of an LLC's organizational and operating capital could be contributed by out-of-state members. Whether the nonresident members are individuals or entities, they could reside in any of the nine non-income-taxing states! Worse yet, there is a collection of tax problems when LLC members reside outside of the U.S. (We'll address foreign residency matters quite fully in Chapter 12.) Now you know one of the reasons why the analysis-of-members portion of Schedule K is so important.

Editorial Note: In alphabetical order, the nine non-income-taxing states are: (1) Alaska, (2) Florida, (3) Nevada, (4) New Hampshire, (5) South Dakota, (6) Tennessee, (7) Texas, (8) Washington, and (9) Wyoming.

Because of nonresidency problems with the collection of its tax, California has promulgated **Form 3832**. Its title is: *Limited Liability Company's List of* [Nonresident] *Members and Consents*. If not already self-evident, the purpose of this form is—

1. To list the names and Tax I.D.s of all LLC members who are not residents of California;

2. To obtain the signatures, where possible, of those nonresidents who consent to the tax jurisdiction of California;

3. To list separately those nonresidents who have sold or transferred their ownership interests during the current year; and

4. To "flag" those who fail to sign the consent statement by requiring the LLC to withhold tax on that member's distributive amount at his highest marginal rate.

For its informative benefit, we present in Figure 6.3 a condensed version of Form 3832. The bulk of the condensation pertains to the various small-print instructions thereon. The consent statement (indicated in bold) is separately cited on page 6-13.

Form 3832	LIST OF NONRESIDENT MEMBERS & CONSENTS		Year
LLC Name	State File No. _____ Fed. Tax I.D. No. _____		

	List Members of Record at End of Taxable Year			
	Name	CONSENT STATEMENT		Tax I.D
		Signature	Date	
1				
2				
3				
4				
5				
etc.				

	List Those Who Sold or Transferred Ownership Interests			
	Name	CONSENT STATEMENT		Tax I.D
		Signature	Date	
1				
2				
3				
etc.				

Fig. 6.3 - General Arrangement of List for Nonresident Member Consents

Immediately below the title, a headnote reads—

For use by LLCs with one or more nonresident members. Attach to Form 568 and give a copy to each nonresident member. Use additional sheet(s) if necessary.

In the signature column, the consent statement reads—

Only nonresident members must sign: "I consent to the jurisdiction of the State of California to tax my distributive share of the LLC income attributable to California sources."

There is also a caution on Form 3832. Every recipient is informed that by signing the form the nonresident is not relieved of his/her/their/its obligation to file California nonresident or part-year resident returns. California bases its filing requirements on the principle of: *Gross income from all sources.* The term "all sources" means (a) within California, (b) outside of California but within the U.S., and (c) outside of the U.S., if so much as $1 is earned from a business in California. The overall consequence is that if an LLC member has to file a federal return and gets an LLC distribution from California, he'll have to file a California return, whether resident or not.

Source Determination Rules

When business income is derived from sources both within and outside of the state, it becomes necessary to determine the portion attributable to California sources. The situation is the same for other business-taxing and income-taxing states. This is a reciprocal agreement among affected states which have adopted the Uniform Division of Income Act for Tax Purposes (in 1967) and the Multistate Tax Compact of 1978. The idea was to avoid double taxation on the same income in one state and distributed to a member in another state, with each state claiming full taxing jurisdiction thereon.

The source determination (origin of income rules) addresses business income and nonbusiness income separately. The term "business income" is directed at a trade or business where extensive personal services are performed on a regular, continuous, and substantial basis. "Nonbusiness income" constitutes all else. Nonbusiness income includes that from real and tangible property (buildings, equipment, vehicles) and from intangible property (bank accounts, stock portfolios, pensions, annuities, royalties).

We summarize in Figure 6.4 the uniform source determination rules. They are "uniform" among the states . . . except for California. Whereas most states use a 3-factor apportionment formula, California uses a 4-factor formula. California does this with **Schedule R** (in Figure 6.4) titled: ***Apportionment and Allocation of Income***. The term "apportionment" means — *the division of business income among states by use of an apportionment formula.* The term "allocation" means— *the assignment of nonbusiness income to a particular state.* Real and tangible property is sourced to the state of its physical presence; intangible property is sourced to the state of each taxpayer's residence.

The standard apportionment formula consists of: (1) a property factor (both real and tangible); (2) a payroll factor (all forms of compensation for personal services rendered); and (3) a sales factor (all gross receipts from the sale of tangible and intangible property). California deviates from this standard by applying a "double-weighted" sales factor. The result is—

$$\left[\frac{\text{Calif. prop.}}{\text{Total prop.}} + \frac{\text{Calif. payroll}}{\text{Total payroll}} + \frac{2 \times \text{Calif. sales}}{\text{Total sales}} \right] \div 4$$

= California Apportionment

The apportionment factor is applied to California-adjusted federal amounts to arrive at a ***California source amount***.

Effect on Schedule K-1(568)

From our earlier comments, you are already aware that each member of an LLC conducting business in California receives a Schedule K-1 (Form 568). This is that ***Member's Share of*** . . . distributive income/payment items. In most every respect except self-employment and foreign tax items, the federal K-1(1065) and the California K-1(568) are item-by-item comparable. The big difference is the number of columns and their headings, and the computational assumptions used by California. The K-1(568)

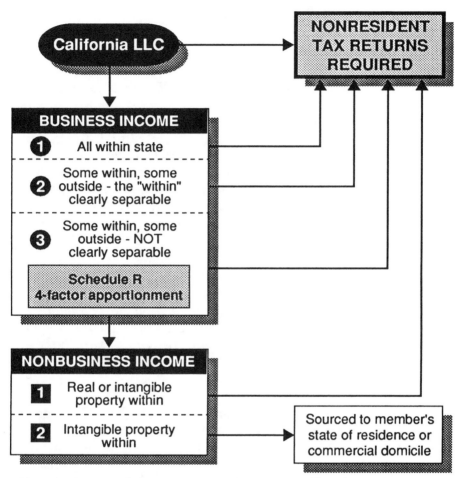

Fig. 6.4 - Source-of-Income Rules for Nonresident Members of Calif. LLC

assumes that each LLC member is a California resident, unless the following question is answered "Yes":

Is this member a nonresident of California? ☐ *Yes* ☐ *No*

The K-1(568) instructions direct that the federal K-1(1065) be used only to prepare column (b) of the K-1(568). The column (b) is captioned: *Amounts from federal K-1(1065)*. Thereafter the K-1(1065) is set aside and the instructions for K-1(568) are to be followed. The LLC is required to furnish each member a copy of the instructions, or at least provide instructions on each item-amount entered in column (b). The column (c) is captioned: *California adjustments*.

The transcriptional focus in Schedule K-1(568) is its columns (**d**) and (**e**). Column (d) is captioned: *Total amounts using California law*. This column is a combination of columns (b): federal amounts and (c): California adjustments. Column (d) is based on the assumption that — temporarily — all members are California residents. This assumption puts all source determinations (origin of income) on common ground. Then column (e) is derived by applying source determination rules (as explained above). Column (e) is captioned: *California source amounts and credits*.

The instructions to column (e) say—

*Column (e) includes **only** income, deductions, gains, or losses that are . . . **sourced to California**. The residency of a member* [at this point] *is not a factor in the amounts to be included in columns (d) and (e). . . . For an LLC doing business wholly within California, columns (d) and (e) will generally be the same . . . except for **nonbusiness intangible income**.* [Emphasis added.]

Nonbusiness intangible income is sourced to the state of residence of a member individual, or to the commercial domicile of a member entity (as per Figure 6.4). The term "nonbusiness intangible income" refers to interest, dividends, capital gains/loss, royalties, and other passive investment income not related directly to the LLC business.

7

PARTNERSHIP LLC RULES

A Partnership Form Of Business Is Most Representative Of An LLC Entity With Two Or More Members. As Each Member Is A Part Owner, Along With Other Part Owners, Those Who Are More Aggressive Will Benefit At The Expense Of Others, Unless Specific Rules Are Meticulously Followed. There Are 29 Such Rules Directed At Tax Liability, Capital Accounting, Basis Accounting, Contributions Of Money And Property, Distributions, Transfers Of Interests, And Adjustments To Basis. All Focus On "Leveling The Field" Between Members And On Assuring That Transactional Ventures Will Have "Economic Substance."

When two or more unincorporated LLC members associate in a profit-seeking venture, they are automatically construed to be a partnership. This is one of the default classification rules discussed previously in Chapter 4. If the members understand the significance of this automatic classification rule, no Form 8832 (Entity Classification Election) is needed. It is only when the members consent to changing their partnership status (as a domestic entity), that Form 8832 is required.

As pointed out in Chapter 1, there is one particular advantage of a partnership. The entity itself is not subject to income tax. True, there is a partnership "return of income" via Form 1065. This is not a tax return; it is an *information* return. The "information" — consisting of ordinary income, rental income, interest, dividends, royalties, capital gains, and other income, gains, losses, credits — is passed through to the individual members of the entity. The pass-through is done on a **prorata sharing** basis. Thereafter, the prorata proceeds are combined with other sources of income on each member's individual Form 1040, and taxed accordingly.

The pass-through and prorata sharing features of a partnership create opportunities for abuse. Such opportunities arise because a partnership is a *flexible economic arrangement* for conducting joint business affairs. Flexibility is tolerated as a means for increasing the efficiency of a business. It is not tolerated as a means for tax shifting, debt avoidance, and accounting misdeeds. To deter starting an LLC partnership on the wrong foot, some 29 statutory tax laws are prescribed. They cover the gamut known as Subchapter K: *Partners and Partnerships* of the Internal Revenue Code (IRC).

Accordingly, what we want to do in this chapter is to overview IRC Subchapter K with you, and point out its highlights that could make your LLC experience both pleasant and lucrative. As in any small business endeavor, dedication, hard work, and self-discipline are essential ingredients. For those who believe that, by being an LLC, a magic wand can be waved and all the arduous tax rules will go away, are in for a surprise. For those who are more realistic, the partnership rules actually make sense. They systematize matters for the orderly conduct of business . . . throughout many years.

Categorizing the 29 Rules

In its present form, IRC Subchapter K: *Partners and Partnerships*, does not mention Limited Liability Companies. As we tried to clarify in Chapter 5, when a two-or-more-member LLC is involved, the return preparer has to check the appropriate "Type of entity" box on Form 1065: *U.S. Return of Partnership Income*. Thereafter, one reads the word "partner" as "LLC member," and the word "partnership" as "limited liability company." For example, Section 701 is titled: *Partners, Not Partnership, Subject to Tax*. One has to read this as: "LLC Members, Not LLC Entity, Subject to Tax." This can make for awkward reading of the partnership rules, unless you acclimate yourself to it. Being an LLC does not invalidate the nearly 50 years (commencing 1956) of partnership tax rules when two or more members engage in entrepreneurial activities.

With these comments in mind, the arrangement of Subchapter K is grouped into six categories, as follows:

A — Determination of Tax Liability }
      Sections 701 through 709 (9 rules) }
      }

B — Contributions to a Partnership }
      Sections 721 through 724 (4 rules) }
      }

C — Distributions by a Partnership }
      Sections 731 through 737 (7 rules) } 29 rules
      }

D — Transfers of Partnership Interests }
      Sections 741 through 743 (3 rules) }
      }

E — Common Accounting Provisions }
      Sections 751 through 755; plus }
      Section 761 (*Terms Defined*) (6 rules) }

By ordinary counting, 701 through 777, it would apear that there are 77 partnership sections (or rules): not the 29 that we state. There is no discrepancy in what we state. There are "gaps" between the sectional groupings. The gaps permit the inclusion of additional laws as needed. One definite such need is the addressing of LLC partnerships in specific LLC terms. Meanwhile, we eliminate the seven rules (771 through 777) that address Electing Large Partnerships. By definition, a "large partnership" is one having 100 or more members in any given year. In an LLC where each member is an owner-manager, we question the likelihood of an LLC partnership ever becoming this large. Consequently, our rule count is reduced to 29.

In Figure 7.1, we present a complete listing of these 29 rules. We urge that you take a moment and read, line by line, the official titles of these rules. By doing so, you'll get a sense of the seriousness expected of you and your associates, when conducting business as an LLC.

Section	Rule Title
INTERNAL REVENUE CODE	
Chapter 1 - Subchapter K - PARTNERS AND PARTNERSHIPS	
Section	Rule Title
A	**Determination of Tax Liability**
701	Partners, Not Partnership, Subject to Tax
702	Income and Credits of Partner
703	Partnership Computations
704	Partner's Distributive Share
705	Determination of Basis of Partner's Interest
706	Taxable Years of Partner and Partnership
707	Transactions Between Partner and Partnership
708	Continuation of Partnership
709	Treatment of Organization and Syndication Fees
B	**Contributions to a Partnership**
721	Nonrecognition of Gain or Loss on Contribution
722	Basis of Contributing Partner's Interest
723	Basis of Property Contributed to Partnership
724	Character of Gain or Loss on Certain Items
C	**Distributions by a Partnership**
731	Extent of Gain or Loss on Distribution
732	Basis of Distributed Property Other Than Money
733	Basis of Distributee Partner's Interest
734	Adjustment to Basis of Undistributed Property
735	Gain or Loss on Disposition of Distributed Property
736	Payments to a Retiring or Deceased Partner
737	Precontribution Gain In Certain Distributions
D	**Transfers of Partnership Interests**
741	Recognition of Gain or Loss on Sale or Exchange
742	Basis of Transferee Partner's Interest
743	Adjustment to Basis of Partnership Property
E	**Common Accounting Provisions**
751	Unrealized Receivables and Inventory Items
752	Treatment of Certain Liabilities
753	Partner Receiving Income In Respect of Decedent
754	Manner of Electing Optional Adjustments
755	Rules for Allocation of Basis
761	Terms Defined

Fig. 7.1 - Basic Tax Rules For Partners & Partnerships

We should tell you that the 29 partnership rules in Figure 7.1 are authoritated in some 670 pages of statutory, regulatory, descriptive, and court-brief text. Altogether, approximately 400,000 words are involved. Obviously, in the 24 pages of this chapter, we can only cover selected highlights. Those that we select are directed at those LLC members who seek to be better informed than they presently are through general hearsay and Internet postings.

The Anti-Abuse Rule

Of the 29 rules listed in Figure 7.1, Section 701 is one of the shortest. It consists of just 35 words. Yet, it is accompanied by nearly 8,000 words of regulations. The most dominant of these regulations (over 7,000 words) is Regulation § 1.701-2: *Anti-abuse rule*. The purpose of this rule is to uphold the for-profit business intent of Section 701 without straying into abusive territory. The implicit intent is to conduct joint business activities (including investments) in a manner that is clearly consistent with all of the income tax provisions of Subchapter K.

The anti-abuse rule is to assure that three particular Section 701 requirements are met. These are:

1. *The partnership must be bona fide and each partnership transaction or series of related transactions . . . must be entered into for a **substantial business purpose**.*

2. *The form of each partnership transaction must be respected under **substance over form** principles.*

3. *The tax consequences . . . to each partner of partnership operations and of transactions between the partner and the partnership must **accurately reflect** the partners' [plural] economic agreement and clearly reflect **each partner's income**.* [Emphasis added.]

As a test of whether an LLC partnership meets these requirements, the regulation asks one pointed question:

*Was the partnership formed with a principal purpose to reduce substantially the present value of the **partners' aggregate federal tax liability** in a manner inconsistent with the intent of subchapter K?* [Emphasis added.]

In other words, is the partnership set up primarily as a tax shelter, a tax shifting vehicle among related taxpayers, a tax maneuvering arrangement between offshore (foreign) and onshore (domestic) members, or a trading pool for members with unused losses that otherwise would be tax wasted?

Numerous factors are taken into consideration before the IRS can make a judgment call on the intent question. Most of these factors are synopsized in Figure 7.2. They are condensed directly from Regulation § 1.701-2(c): *Facts and circumstances analysis; factors.* We show seven of such factors.

If the IRS decides that an LLC partnership is primarily tax motivated rather than being business motivated, it can disregard the arrangement in its entirety. The partners are then restored to their individual capacities without any pass-through or prorata sharing benefits whatsoever.

Economic Substance Rule

Section 704 is titled: *Partner's Distributive Share.* Its subsections (a) and (b) are titled, respectively: *Effect of Partnership Agreement* and *Determination of Distributive Share.* The substance of these two subsections is that—

A partner's distributive share of income, gain, loss, deduction, or credit shall . . . be determined by the partnership agreement . . . [OR] in accordance with the partner's [capital] interest in the partnership . . . if the allocation does not have substantial economic effect.

This statutory wording is the economic substance rule for prorata sharing. The "economic substance" — or, substantial economic effect — derives from each member's capital interest (money and property) in the LLC arrangement. The economic

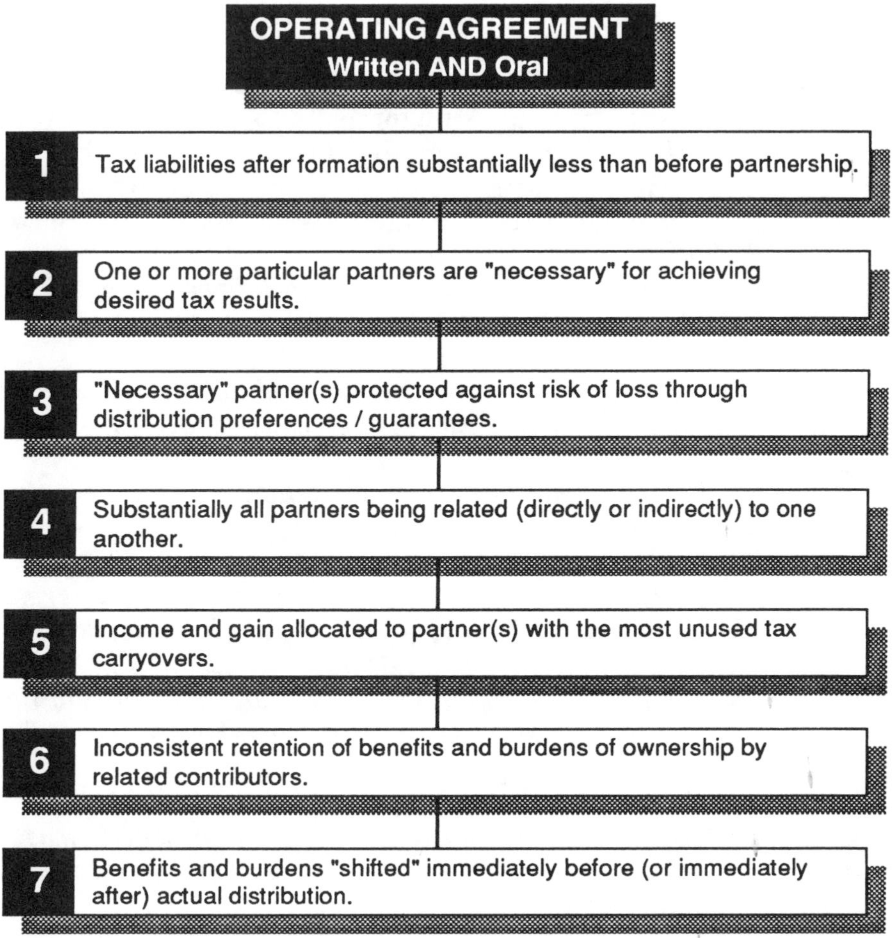

OPERATING AGREEMENT
Written AND Oral

1	Tax liabilities after formation substantially less than before partnership.
2	One or more particular partners are "necessary" for achieving desired tax results.
3	"Necessary" partner(s) protected against risk of loss through distribution preferences / guarantees.
4	Substantially all partners being related (directly or indirectly) to one another.
5	Income and gain allocated to partner(s) with the most unused tax carryovers.
6	Inconsistent retention of benefits and burdens of ownership by related contributors.
7	Benefits and burdens "shifted" immediately before (or immediately after) actual distribution.

Fig. 7.2 - Factors Indicative of Tax Motivation Over Business Motivation

benefits and economic burdens from the partnership operations must flow through proportionately to the ownership interests in the venture. If member A's ownership interest is $10,000, for example, and member B has a $30,000 interest, the flow through of benefits and burdens should be (approximately) 25% to member A and 75% to member B [10,000 ÷ 40,000; 30,000 ÷ 40,000]. We say "approximately" because there does not have to be a dollar-for-dollar correlation if the partnership agreement provides otherwise.

The "otherwise", however, must satisfy the *substantial economic effect* test. Why would member A, for example, get only 10% of the benefits, and carry 50% of the burdens? With a 25% ownership interest, member A might agree to accept 20% of the benefits and 30% of the burdens in deference to member B's superior knowledge, contacts, and personal service devotion to the business. How much stretch is there, when trying to achieve substantial economic effect?

The term "substantial economic effect" is defined in Regulation § 1.704-1(b)(2) and its subparagraphs. Pertinent portions read—

*A partner will have economic effect **if, and only if,** throughout the full term of the partnership, the agreement provides—*

(1) For determination and maintenance of the partners' [plural] capital accounts,

*(2) Upon liquidation of . . . any partner's interest, distributions are required to be made in accordance with the **positive capital account balances** of all the partners, . . . after taking into account all capital account adjustments for the partnership, and*

*(3) If such [liquidating] partner has **a deficit balance** in his capital account . . ., he is **unconditionally obligated to restore** the amount of such deficit balance to the partnership.*

*The economic effect of an allocation (or allocations) is substantial if there is a reasonable possibility that the allocation (or allocations) will **substantially affect the dollar amounts** to be received by the partners from the partnership, independent of tax consequences.* [Emphasis added.]

In other words, if member C puts up $10,000 and walks away from the partnership with $100,000 in benefits and no burdens, there is no economic substance. Particularly so if member D puts up $50,000 and gets only $10,000 in benefits while being stuck with

$90,000 in burdens. This kind of arrangement is not a bona fide partnership; it is a sham. Member C is a con artist. Such artistry can be prevalent in any joint venture, whether an LLC or not. The intrigue of the letters "LL": *Limited Liability*, can be disarming.

Maintaining Capital Accounts

In principal, all LLC members are treated equally on a per capita basis. This means that if the total capitalization of the partnership is $100,000, for example, the allocation (of income, gain, loss, deduction, or credit) to each partner is proportional to his/her/its capital account balance. For good reason and cause, the partnership agreement may provide for different allocations than the per capita prorations. Nevertheless, it is each partner's capital account balance (at the end of each prescribed accounting period for the partnership) that determines the economic effect on the allocation process.

Therefore, determining and maintaining each partner's capital account (**within** the partnership) is *key* to successful partnership operation. The "determination" aspect thereof turns primarily on the fair market value of property, other than money, that is contributed to the partnership. Money is money, and is valued at whatever denomination is on its face. But valuing property is a different matter altogether. The term "property" includes such variant items as real estate, natural resource interests, machinery, equipment, vehicles, materials and supplies, merchandise inventory, accounts receivable, mortgage notes, promissory notes, private securities, negotiable securities, commodities (gold, wheat, oil), fractional interests in other entities, and so on. Needless to say, market valuing fairly such a wide variety of property items can be a contentious and drawn-out issue. It can become a war zone among serious contributors, con artists, and sophisticated schemers.

For official guidance, we turn to Regulation § 1.704-1(b)(2)(iv)(h): *Determinations of fair market value*. Excerpted portions from this regulation read—

The fair market value assigned to property . . . will be regarded as correct, provided that (1) such value is reasonably agreed to among the partners in arm's-length negotiations, (2) the partners have sufficiently adverse interests . . . and (3) the valuation . . . [is] on a property-by-property basis.

The above relates the determination of a member's *contributions* to his capital account. Maintaining such an account is another matter. The "maintenance" aspect deals with **adjustments** to each account throughout the partnership's operating year. For this aspect, Regulation § 1.704-1(b)(2)(iv)(a): *Maintenance of capital accounts*, is instructive. Our position is that this regulation should be mandatory in every LLC operating agreement.

The pertinent portions of the maintenance regulation read—

The partners' [plural] capital accounts will be considered to be determined and maintained . . . if, and only if, each partner's [singular] capital account is increased by—

(1) *the amount of money contributed by him to the partnership,*
(2) *the fair market value of property contributed by him, and*
(3) *allocation to him of partnership income and gain (including allocations exempt from tax . . . and adjustments* [amortization, depreciation, depletion] *to reflect book values)*

and is decreased by—

(4) *the amount of money distributed to him by the partnership,*
(5) *the fair market value of property distributed to him,*
(6) *allocation to him of expenditures and liabilities of the partnership, and*
(7) *allocations of any partnership loss and deduction.*

The message above, and in Figure 7.3, is that a lot of capital accounting discipline is required when getting an LLC partnership up and running. Implied in this discipline is that there must be enough capital reserves on hand to meet the liabilities of a

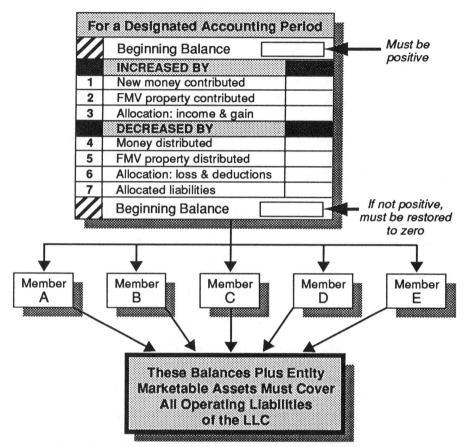

Fig. 7.3 - Mechanics of Partners' Capital Accounting for a Solvent LLC

partnership LLC, as distinguished from the personal liabilities of each member.

For good capital accounting discipline, keep one point foremost in mind. Each member's capital account within the partnership is NOT his private piggy bank. It is not a cash kitty from which a member may withdraw or borrow money at will. A positive capital balance must be maintained by each member at all times. The moment any member starts behaving cavalierly about his obligation for maintaining a positive balance, that's the time to prepare to cut him loose and terminate his interests in the partnership. Promised restoration of capital deficits are difficult to enforce legally, particularly in an LLC.

Mandatory Allocation of Debt

Technically, all debt of an LLC partnership is *nonrecourse*. The term "nonrecourse" means that no member can be held personally responsible for repayment of partnership (the entity) debts. Such debts include accounts payable (to suppliers, venders, contractors, etc.), and delinquent payroll, if any. As nonrecourse debts, they lack economic substance. The creditors, lenders, and employees will suffer the economic loss if the partnership does not have sufficient funds to repay its nonrecourse obligations. As a consequence, all LLC arrangements tend to be suspect. Creditors, lenders, and employees worry about getting paid. They want some form of "guarantee" that the LLC partnership will pay them.

The most credible form of guarantee for an LLC is a mandatory allocation of partnership debt to each LLC member. The allocation mandate must be spelled out in the operating agreement of the entity. Said agreement is filed with state authorities, where the LLC permit was issued. This makes the allocation legally enforceable, proportionately, upon each LLC member. As we have mentioned previously, an LLC is not — repeat, NOT — an arrangement for defrauding creditors of monies properly due them in the normal course of business. As depicted in Figure 7.4, the LLC situation differs substantially from that of a regular partnership. In a regular partnership, any one general partner can be held personally liable for all partnership debt. He, in turn, can take legal action against other general partners. In an LLC, a creditor or creditors can recover only the per-member allocated debt amount. This means legal action against all LLC members simultaneously, for each's allocated share of the aggregate partnership debt.

How are allocations attributable to nonrecourse debt determined?

Regulation § 1.704-2: *Nonrecourse liabilities*, addresses this point specifically. Unfortunately, it is a 15,000-word regulation. The allocation is based on a *minimum gain chargeback* principle. The "minimum gain" is established (as of a given date) by treating all LLC nonrecourse debt as having been fully discharged for its fair

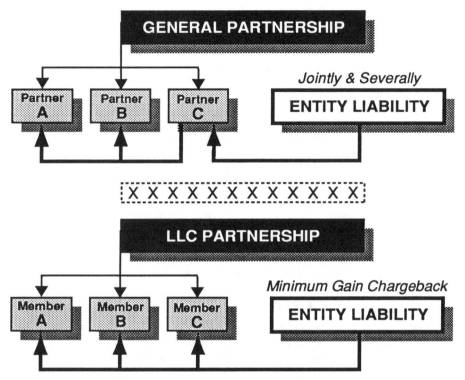

Fig. 7.4 - Liability Comparison Between General & LLC Partnerships

market value. To the extent that this amount exceeds the aggregate marketable assets of the partnership, there is, constructively, minimum gain. This gain is charged back to each LLC member in proportion to his capital interests in the partnership. The chargeback process creates economic substance out of the excess nonrecourse debt. This is because each LLC member now bears his proportionate share of the economic burdens of the enterprise.

Consider, for example, that the total nonrecourse debt of an LLC partnership is $100,000. The entity assets available for discharging that debt is $80,000. The minimum gain thereby is $20,000. Suppose there were three LLC members with capital interests of 50%, 35%, and 15%. Their respective chargeback amounts would be $10,000; $7,000; and $3,000. These amounts are subtracted from each member's capital account balances (in Figure 7.3). If any negative capital balance occurs, the negative must be restored to zero via additional capital contributions from the affected member. IRS regulations allow 90 days in which to restore any negative capital account balance to zero. If this is not done, the partnership is deemed to be abusive, and subject to reallocation of interests.

Partnership Accounting Year

Ordinarily, a business entity is permitted to set up its books and records to mirror its "natural business cycle." The idea is to include the full range of ups and downs of income and expenses throughout a 12-month period. This is called the "accounting year" of the business. It can be any 12 months starting January 1st, February 1st, March 1st, . . . December 1st. If starting other than on January 1st, the cycle is a *fiscal year*.

Individuals, generally, must file their income tax returns on a *calendar* year basis. If a partnership files its "return of income" on a fiscal year basis, and its partners file on a calendar year, can you not sense the overlapping of accounting items between the entity and the individuals' returns? There is also opportunity for intentional income deferral by structuring the accounting overlappings.

Suppose, for example, that a partnership's tax year ended on January 31. A calendar-year partner's income allocation from the partnership would be reported by the partner in his tax year ending on December 31. This produces an 11-month deferral of income recognition to the LLC member.

To prevent the deferral and distortion of income, gain, loss, deduction, or credit between partners and their partnership, IRC Section 706 applies. This section is titled: ***Taxable Years of Partner and Partnership***. The substance of this 1,300-word mandate is that the LLC partnership must conform its tax year to the tax years of its owners. Three "tests" are used for determining the tax years of the entity owners. These are—

(1) Majority interests: those LLC members having more than 50% ownership of profits and capital.

(2) All principal members: each of whom has at least a 5% interest in the profits and capital.

(3)   Least aggregate deferral of income to all members (determined by a quite complex weighting formula).

Our position is that, in an LLC partnership, most owners most likely would be individuals. Hence, the most practical procedure is to adopt a calendar accounting year for the partnership. This simplifies allocation and pass-through matters greatly. Also, it helps to thwart IRS suspicion of using the partnership improperly.

An exception to "our" calendar year rule is provided in subsection 706(b)(1)(C): ***Business Purpose***. This subsection reads in part—

A partnership may have a [fiscal] *taxable year . . . if it establishes, to the satisfaction of the* [IRS], *a business purpose therefor. Any deferral of income to its partners shall not be treated as a business purpose.*

To establish a business purpose, the LLC partnership must file Form 1128: ***Application to Adopt, Change, or Retain a Tax Year***. This form comprises four full-size pages, over 60 checkboxes, and over 6,000 words of instruction. Take a look at the official form yourself. If you do, you and your LLC associates will be more than anxious to adopt a calendar accounting year for the partnership.

Changes in Members' Interests

LLC members come and go. They want to get in; they want to get out. Some want to increase their capital interests; some want to decrease said interests. Some want to sell or exchange their interests to new members. Some retire; some gift their interests to family members; and some die. What else can you expect of human beings when putting their capital and talents on the line. Still, what effect do these varying ownership interests have on the partnership operation?

Needless to say, all such changes affect the internal accounting of the partnership. Particularly, the allocable sharing aspects. Does a member who enters on October 18th with a $10,000 contribution get a full year's sharing of the distributive items (income, gain, loss, deduction, credit)? Of course not. He gets 75 days' worth of allocation (365 – 290 days from January 1 through October 17). Or, suppose a high-roller member wants out on January 15th. Does he get a full year's allocation of the shared items? Again, of course not. He gets only 15 days' worth of allocation (January 1 through January 15). In other words, as members come and go, the role of **participant days** takes on an accounting importance of its own.

As per subsection 706(d): *Determination of Distributive Share When Partner's Interest Changes*, the LLC partnership may use—

> *any method prescribed . . . which takes into account the varying interests of the partners in the partnership during [its] taxable year.*

This statutory authority leads to accounting in *dollar days* as well as in *membership days*. Can you not imagine the distributive sharing complexity when members come and go in an undisciplined way?

LLC partnerships particularly attract shrewd and cunning members. Such persons are the type who want everything in their favor. They seek to time their entry into and withdrawal from the partnership just before *and* just after a major partnership transaction takes place. For example, the partnership sells its small shopping center for $1,000,000. After taking into account the partnership's adjusted basis in the property and its selling expenses, the partnership's capital gain is $600,000, say. Just 10 days before the sale, a shrewd member plunks down $100,000 as additional contribution to his existing capital. As of the date of sale, he has a 50% ownership interest in the partnership. Just 10 days after the sale, he withdraws his $100,000 and demands $300,000 of the capital gain as his "distributive share" of the proceeds. Come on, now: $300,000 for a 20-day voluntary loan to the partnership. How unreasonable can one be? Nevertheless, if the demands are not met immediately, the egregious member threatens to get an attorney and tear apart the partnership agreement. He already knows that the agreement has no prohibition whatsoever against his 20-day incursion strategy. He knows this because it was *he* who diverted attention from any such provision in the agreement.

There is really only one way to handle the above matter and others like it. Limit a member's entry into, and withdrawal from, the LLC partnership to specific accounting-period ending dates: March 31, June 30, or September 30, for example. Furthermore, limit participation in entity transactional gains or losses to the percentage of days a partner participated during the total holding-period days that the property was owned by the partnership.

Let us illustrate. Suppose that in the 20-day incursion example above, the shopping center was held by the partnership for 1,000 days before it was sold. The percentage of incursion participation in the property holding would be 10 days divided by 1,000 days, or 1%. He gets no transaction credit for remaining in the partnership for 10 days after the property was sold. Thus, instead of the $300,000 he demanded by threatening a lawsuit, he would be entitled to just 1% or $3,000 only. Does **your** LLC partnership agreement cover situations like this?

Basis & Adjustments Thereto

The term "basis" (as you already know) is a *tax reference* for establishing the amount of gain or loss from a property transaction. One's basis includes his acquisition cost of the property, plus added items of cost while holding the property, minus statutory adjustments, such as depreciation, depletion, etc. Special basis rules apply when property is acquired by gift, inheritance, exchange, or assumption of a prior owner's debt. The basis rules of general application are found in Subchapter O of the Internal Revenue Code: *Gain or Loss on Disposition of Property*. Some 30 such rules (Sections 1011 – 1060) are prescribed. The key one is Section 1011: *Adjusted Basis for Determining Gain or Loss*. All are beyond our discussion here. We reference them only to have you focus on **property dispositions**.

A "property disposition" occurs when an LLC member transfers his ownership interests in a property item to a partnership with others. Immediately before the transfer takes place, the contributing member has a tax basis in that property. If, instead of transferring the property to the partnership, it were sold to a party outside of the partnership, gain or loss would be tax recognized at that time. But when contributing property to a partnership, no immediate gain or loss is tax recognized [Section 721].

Meanwhile, when a member contributes money and property to a partnership, he does so for the express purpose of acquiring (purchasing) an ownership interest therein. Such an interest is a capital asset. Unless the contributor pays all cash, what appears to be an accounting anomaly develops. His tax basis in his ownership interest will differ — often substantially —from his capital basis in the partnership. Here's an example of this "anomaly."

A member buys a $100,000 capital interest in a partnership. To do this, he conveys to the partnership $20,000 in money and property whose fair market value is $80,000. His tax basis in the property is $45,000. This amount includes a $40,000 mortgage on the property which the contributing member is obligated to pay. At this point, his tax basis in his $100,000 ownership interest in the partnership is $65,000 ($20,000 cash plus $45,000 basis in property). Let us continue.

Once title to the $80,000 property item is taken over by the partnership, the property belongs to all members of the LLC. In our case, suppose that three other members assumed $30,000 of the contributing member's $40,000 mortgage debt. His tax basis in the property is now reduced to $15,000 ($45,000 initially minus $30,000 of his mortgage debt assumed by others). At this point, he has an *adjusted* tax basis of $35,000 ($20,000 money plus $15,000 basis in property) in a partnership interest worth $100,000. Doesn't sound right, does it?

But it is right. Had the contributing member subsequently liquidated his $100,000 partnership interest for $100,000 cash, he would pay tax on $65,000 ($100,000 liquidating value minus $35,000 adjusted tax basis).

As partnership operational time and activities go on, a member's adjusted tax basis in his partnership interest can, and often does, change. If he contributes additional money, or contributes property which has a basis different from its market value, his tax basis in his partnership interest will increase. Conversely, if he takes money or property out of the partnership, his tax basis will decrease. If there is an allocation to him of income or gain from the partnership operation, he pays tax on that allocation. If, upon paying the tax, he lets the allocated amounts "roll over" in the partnership (without withdrawing them), his adjusted tax basis will increase.

Somewhere down the road, a member recovers his adjusted tax base. When he does so, it is called: *return of capital*. Said return is tax FREE!

Whose responsibility is it to keep track of the various adjustments to a member's tax basis in his LLC partnership interest? It is **not** the responsibility of the partnership. The partnership has its own basis accounting problems. The responsibility rests solely and exclusively with each LLC member. If, as an LLC member, you do not keep comprehensive basis records on your own, the IRS will assert that your tax basis is zero. From such time on, you are ineligible for return of any capital, tax free. The partnership has to report all distributions made to you, to the IRS.

Partnership Basis Accounting

When one or more items of property are contributed by one or more LLC members to a partnership, the property or properties take on a new basis. The partnership, as an entity, now owns the property. It accepts the contributed property at its fair market value as though it had acquired the property by purchase. From then on, there may be additions to the property, subtractions from it, adjustments to it, or debt encumbrances placed on it.

The net result is that there develops an "inside basis" to property accounting — item by item. This basis accounting is separate and distinct from any outside basis that a member may have. When a partnership property item is sold to a nonpartner person or entity, income gain or loss is accounting recognized by the partnership. The partnership income and gain are passed through allocably to each partner where it is income taxed.

As you should sense by now, inside basis and outside basis accounting can become complex indeed. Much depends on the relative value of money and property contributed to the partnership; the diversity and use of property items; the number of contributing members; the relative capital interests of the members in the partnership; and the distributions of property to the members without its being sold by the partnership. The best we can do in general terms is the depiction we present in Figure 7.5. We just want you to visualize the separate basis accounting roles of the LLC members and their LLC partnership.

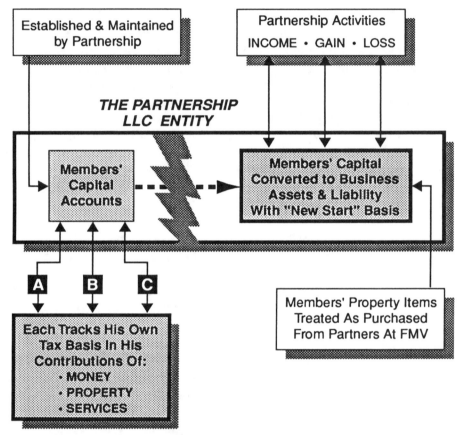

Fig. 7.5 - Separate Accounting Between LLC Members & Their Partnership

As justification for our Figure 7.5, we suggest that you glance back at Figure 7.1 (on page 7-4) for a moment. Of the 29 listings there, 10 have the word "basis" in their titles. The 10 basis sections are—

Sec. 705 — Determination of *Basis* of Partner's Interest
Sec. 722 — *Basis* of Contributing Partner's Interest
Sec. 723 — *Basis* of Property Contributed to Partnership

Sec. 732	— *Basis* of Distributed Property Other Than Money
Sec. 733	— *Basis* of Distributee Partner's Interest
Sec. 734	— Optional Adjustment to *Basis* of Undistributed Partnership Property
Sec. 742	— *Basis* of Transferee Partner's Interest
Sec. 743	— Optional Adjustment to *Basis* of Partnership Property
Sec. 754	— Manner of Electing Optional Adjustment to *Basis* of Partnership Property
Sec. 755	— Rules for Allocation of *Basis*

Related to, but omitted from the above 10 basis sections, are Section 721: *Nonrecognition of Gain or Loss on Contribution*; Section 731: *Extent of Recognition of Gain or Loss on Distribution*; and Section 741: *Recognition and Character of Gain or Loss on Sale or Exchange* (of one member's interest to another member in the LLC partnership). These three gain or loss sections highlight the significance of basis accounting and tracking for property disposition to, from, within, and outside the partnership arrangement. Accordingly, we touch on each one of these three sections separately below.

Contributions TO Partnership LLC

Section 721: *Nonrecognition of Gain or Loss on Contribution*, states the obvious. No gain or loss is tax recognized either to the partnership LLC or to any of its members upon the contribution of property, including money, to the partnership. This nonrecognition aspect derives from characterizing the contributory transaction as an equal-value **exchange**. That is, a member exchanges money and property for an *ownership interest* in the partnership. The value of his ownership interest in dollars is exactly the same as that of the money and property (at fair market value) contributed. The rule applies whether a new partnership is being formed or an existing partnership is seeking new capital.

Let us illustrate this nonrecognition/nontaxable concept in the simplest of terms. A member-to-be contributes property worth $10,000 to a partnership in exchange for a $10,000 ownership interest therein. His basis in that property is $4,000. Had he sold the property to a nonpartner, he would have had to pay tax on a $6,000 gain ($10,000 value − $4,000 basis). Instead, the tax is deferred until his partnership interest itself is disposed of . . . whenever. Thus, the partnership has received "built-in gain" property. But this has tax meaning only to the LLC member.

Conversely, property is contributed which has a market value of $4,000 and a tax basis of $10,000. There is a "built-in loss" here of $6,000 ($4,000 value − $10,000 basis). This, too, is not tax recognized until the member's ownership interest in the partnership is liquidated.

The Section 721 nonrecognition-on-contribution rule is modified in two situations. As an example of the first situation, suppose that in the $10,000 built-in gain property above, instead of a $10,000 ownership interest, the contributor received an $8,000 ownership interest. An amount of $2,000 in cash was returned to him. He pays tax on $1,200 of said amount [$2,000 proceeds minus (2/10 x $4,000 basis)]. His adjusted basis in the $8,000 partnership interest is now $3,200 [$4,000 minus (2/10 x $4,000 recognized basis)].

The second situation modifying Section 721 is where personal services are contributed in lieu of money or property. For example, an existing member's ownership interest is $8,000 (with a basis of $5,000). He has performed personal services to the partnership equivalent to $2,000 gross pay. Instead of receiving a paycheck for this amount, he wants to exchange it for a $2,000 additional capital interest. He can do this, of course, but **not** tax free. He has to pay income tax and social security/medicare tax on the entire $2,000. When he does so, his tax basis in his now $10,000 ownership interest is increased by $2,000 (from $5,000 basis to $7,000).

Distributions FROM Partnership LLC

Section 731: *Extent of Recognition of Gain or Loss on Distribution*, addresses the gain or loss recognition on distributions of partnership property. The law itself is comprised of about 1,200 statutory words. It is accompanied by some 4,000 regulatory words plus over 13,000 words of explanatory text by leading tax authorities. It is truly a formidable accounting and analysis task to distinguish between those distributions which are taxable and those which are not taxable. All that we can do here, therefore, is to synopsize the general principles underlying Section 731.

First off, there are two types of distributions from a partnership to its partners. There are *current* distributions and *liquidating* distributions. A current distribution is that which is made from the earnings and profits generated by the partnership. These distributions are taxable, or at least, tax accountable. A liquidating distribution is a redemption of part or all of a member's ownership interest in the partnership. Whether made periodically or in a lump sum, all distributions are treated as having been made at the end of the partnership's taxable accounting year.

In the most generalized sense possible, distributions of ownership capital (money and property) are not taxable except to the extent that the amount of money or marketable securities exceeds the member's adjusted basis in the partnership capital.

Section 731(a)(1) makes it clear that when any money is distributed that exceeds a member's adjusted basis in the partnership (immediately before the distribution) it is taxable. The problem is, the term "money" means more than a check made payable from the partnership's bank account. The term includes marketable securities (actively traded financial instruments). The term also includes *constructive cash distributions.* Constructive cash occurs when a member's share of partnership liabilities is reduced; when the partnership cancels a loan owed to it by a member; when the partnership expends funds on a member's behalf; and when a nonpartner owing money to the partnership instead pays it directly to a member. All of these constructive cash distributions are taxable as ordinary income to the distributee member. The partnership, therefore, must take heed and report correctly to the IRS all such monetary distributions.

Distributions of property are another matter. Where a distribution consists solely of property *other than* money, constructive cash, or marketable securities, it generally will not produce taxable gain or loss for the member. Instead, the gain or loss inherent in the property is deferred until the member actually sells or exchanges it with a nonpartner. The distributee member is on the "honor system" to preserve his tax basis in said property.

Transfer of Partnership Interest

A partnership interest is a *unit of property* in and of its own. It is some determinable fraction or percentage of the total capitalization of the business. Suppose, for example, that an LLC member's interest is 30% of the partnership's capital. He can sell all or a portion of this to an existing member. Or, he can sell to an outsider who becomes a member by purchase of all or part of the 30% interest. This is not an exchange in the sense of a distributional liquidation between partnership and member. It is a transaction solely between one LLC member and another LLC member. It's fully tax recognized to the selling member. This is the essence of Section 741: *Recognition and Character of Gain or Loss on Sale or Exchange* of partnership interest.

Section 741 goes on to say—

Such gain or loss shall be . . . from the sale or exchange of a capital asset, except as otherwise provided in section 751 (relating to unrealized receivables and inventory items).

In other words, when selling a partnership interest to another LLC member, the "unit of property" being transferred has *two* tax characteristics. One is that of a capital asset: called Section 1221 property (*Capital Asset Defined*). The second characteristic is ordinary income property: called Section 751 (*Unrealized Receivables and Inventory Items*). The term "unrealized receivables" means goods delivered or to be delivered, or services rendered or to be rendered, to the extent not previously included in income. The term "inventory items" means items on hand at the close of the taxable year held primarily for sale to customers.

Thus, the transferring member's tax basis in his partnership interest has to be apportioned between Section 1221 property and Section 751 property comparable to that which exists in the partnership itself. Section 1221 property gets capital gain/loss treatment, whereas Section 751 property gets ordinary income/loss treatment.

8

NOT-FOR-PROFIT RULES

As A Pass-Through Entity, A Partnership LLC Is Subject To The Profit Motivation Tests Of Section 183: "Activities Not Engaged In For Profit." There Are NINE Such Tests. Collectively, Their Objective Is To X-Ray Into The Minds Of LLC Participants To Determine Their Real Motivation. The PRESUMPTION Is That Unless A Net Profit Is Realized In 3-Out-Of-5 Consecutive Years, The LLC Activity Could Well Be A Tax Shelter Or Other Deceptive Arrangement For Substantially Understating Income Tax. The Presumption Can Be Rebutted With Real Facts And Circumstances That Demonstrate Economic Substance And Genuine Risk.

Partnerships, S corporations, and trusts all have one thing in common. They are used as tax shelters and other arrangements for understating tax liabilities, claiming excessive deductions, generating artificial losses, and for pursuing other deceptive practices — some quite sophisticated — for avoiding income, gift, and estate taxation. The feature that creates such possibilities is that the entity itself is not taxed. The pass-through aspects can be gerrymandered to give the participants tax advantages which were never intended. The gerrymandering applies also to single-member LLCs, but the opportunities for abuse are not as prevalent as in the case of partnership LLCs with multiple members.

The IRS classifies a pass-through entity as a tax shelter when the aggregate pass-throughs produce a *substantial understatement* of income tax. Such an understatement occurs when the amount of tax reported on a return is more than 10% (or $5,000) of the tax required to be shown (as determined by the IRS). Within this framework, a tax shelter is statutorily defined as—

(1)   a partnership or other entity,
(2)   any investment plan or arrangement, or
(3)   any other plan or arrangement,

if a significant purpose . . . is the avoidance or evasion of Federal income tax [IRC Sec. 6662(d)(2)(C)(iii)].

To address the deceptive practices of any tax shelter-type arrangement, IRC Section 183 applies. This section is titled: *Activities Not Engaged in for Profit.* The idea is a presumption that, unless the venture produces a net profit in 3 out of 5 years of operation, it is tax suspect. Under this presumption, all deductions and expenses in excess of gross income are disallowed. The nature and purpose of the activity is then scrutinized. Objective tests are applied that X-ray the minds of the principals for determining whether the enterprise is genuinely motivated for profit purposes.

Do the Section 183 rules apply to LLCs? They most certainly do! Because of the relative newness of LLCs (circa 1997), Section 183 itself does not specifically address LLCs. But it is very clear from IRS and Court interpretations, that the not-for-profit aspects of Section 183 apply to "any arrangement" that might give rise to an understatement of tax. An LLC is no exception. Accordingly, in this chapter we want to familiarize you with the various not-for-profit rules that may have escaped inclusion in your LLC organizational "plan."

Suspect Patterns

The principle of economic substance plays a dominant role in the tax legitimacy of any entity with more than one participant. The bonafideness of this role can be identified initially by certain "patterns" that can be observed. If an LLC arrangement exhibits any of these patterns, the LLC becomes tax suspect.

What are the suspect patterns? There are four, as follows:

Pattern 1 — The activity is not engaged in for profit, but all of its aspects have economic substance. Result: Deductions arising from the activity are allowable to the extent that they do not exceed the gross income from the activity.

This is the typical hobby loss situation rather than a tax shelter situation. The expenditures are actual, the debts (if any) are real, and assets are purchased for their real value. But the facts are that the taxpayer never expected or intended to make a profit. This is the classic not-for-profit premise underlying Section 183.

Pattern 2 — All aspects of a purported activity are without economic substance and the activity is a sham. Result: No deductions are allowable.

No deductions are allowed because there is no investment, no indebtedness, and no expense. It is unnecessary to ask if the activity was engaged in for profit, because there was no activity. The "activity" is nothing more than sophisticated tax evasion

Pattern 3 — The activity as a whole is engaged in for profit, but certain aspects thereof *do not have* economic substance. Result: The deductions attributable to the lack of economic substance are disallowed. Other deductions are allowable in full.

This is the situation where the activity generates economic profit, but the taxpayer — by virtue of purported investments that lack economic substance — reports a substantial tax loss. It's the turning of a good economic deal into a paper tax loss.

Pattern 4 — The activity as a whole is not engaged in for profit, but certain aspects *do have* economic substance. Result: The deductions attributable to those aspects having economic substance are allowed to the extent provided under Section 183. All other deductions are disallowed.

This is a typical tax shelter situation. When seen as a whole, it is not engaged in for profit, but there are certain out-of-pocket expenditures. These actual expenditures cannot be said to lack economic substance. Yet they are incurred in an activity in which the taxpayer did not intend to make an economic profit.

> *Editorial Note*: The thumbnail digests of the four patterns above are lifted directly from *CCH Standard Federal Tax Reporter*; Vol. 4 (2002); page 26,785: *Basic tax shelter patterns.*

When any of these patterns radiate from an LLC within a three-consecutive-year period, tax sensitive antenna go up. Then the IRS comes on board to investigate.

"Not-for-Profit" Defined

Section 183(c) gives a 30-word definition of what constitutes a not-for-profit activity. We think a more instructional definition is that prescribed by IRS Regulation § 1.183-2(a). It consists of about 300 words and is titled: *Activity Not Engaged in for Profit Defined*. We present this regulation in two parts, separately, and add our interpretation of where the IRS is coming from.

The first part of Regulation § 1.183-2(a) reads—

*For purposes of Section 183 . . ., the term "activity not engaged in for profit" means **any activity other than** one with respect to which deductions are allowable for the taxable year under section 162 or . . . section 212. Deductions are allowable under section 162 for expenses of **carrying on** activities which constitute a trade or business of the taxpayer and under section 212 for expenses **in connection with** activities engaged in for the production or collection of income or for the management, conservation, or maintenance of property held for the production of income. . . . Deductions are not allowable under section 162 or 212 for activities which are carried on primarily as a sport, hobby, or recreation. [Emphasis added.]*

The reference to Section 162 (*Trade or Business Expenses*) and 212 (*Expenses for Production of Income*) is to call to your attention "livelihood businesses." The premise is that, if your LLC is engaged in a Section 162 or Section 212 activity, your sole motivation is profit making. If you do not realize a spendable profit after a reasonable length of time, you shut the business down. You either go into another business or seek employment in one which does make a profit. Your livelihood — food, rent, mortgage, insurance, utilities, clothing, etc. — depends on it. If your LLC does not realistically qualify under Sections 162 or 212, you automatically come under the provision of Section 183.

The second part of Regulation § 1.183-2(a) reads—

*The determination on whether an activity is engaged in for profit is to be made **by reference to objective standards**, taking into account all of the facts and circumstances of each case. Although a reasonable expectation of profit is not required, the facts and circumstances must indicate that the taxpayer **entered into** the activity, **or continued** the activity, **with the objective** of making a profit. In determining whether such an objective exists, it may be sufficient that there is a small chance of making a large profit. . . . Greater weight is given to objective facts than to the taxpayer's mere statement of his intent.*

This portion of the regulation is trying to tell you that even if your activity is, by definition, Section 183 (not-for-profit), you may still get your losses deducted if your *objective* is to make a profit. Determining said objective is not based on your own statements of intent. It is based on all of the facts and circumstances of your entering into and continuing your activity. It is as though the IRS has a special X-ray machine that can look inside an LLC mind to determine its real motivation. Buzz words, slick promotional clauses, and creative business models are ignored.

"Relevant Factors" Listed

The objective criteria for determining your profit motive are listed in Regulation § 1.183-2(b): *Relevant factors.* These are determinative factors which the various courts — over a period of many years — have agreed are indicative of your underlying

motives. If you meet all of the qualifying tests, the presumption —
for the year (or years) in question only — is that your activity is
engaged in for profit. Whether you actually make a profit each year
is another matter. Not making a profit may be attributable to factors
beyond your control, so long as you try to surmount them.

There are **nine** relevant factors cited in Regulation § 1.183-2(b).
The preamble to this listing reads as follows:

> *In determining whether an activity is engaged in for profit, all
> facts and circumstances with respect to the activity are to be
> taken into account. **No one factor is determinative in making
> this determination**. In addition, it is not intended that only the
> factors described in this paragraph are to be taken into account
> . . ., or that a determination is to be made on the basis that the
> number of factors (whether or not listed in this paragraph)
> indicating a lack of profit objective exceeds the number of
> factors indicating a profit objective, or vice versa. Among the
> factors which should normally be taken into account are—*

What does this regulatory preamble say? It says that if five or
more of the nine relevant factors are in your favor, your activity may
still be judged as not-for-profit. The "vice versa" says that if you
fail five or more of the nine factors, you could be judged for profit.
This is the legalese way of saying that, although your profit motive
is determined by nine objective factors, the determiner — the IRS or
Tax Court (or other court) — can apply subjective analysis (personal
judgment) when arriving at its conclusion. In other words, the nine
factors are not tallied in scoreboard fashion.

What are the nine objective factors? In abbreviated fashion, they
are listed in Figure 8.1 sequentially as they appear in Regulation §
1.183-2(b)(1)-(9). We will address each factor separately.

Your Manner & Expertise

The first two factors in Figure 8.1 are captioned in Regulation §
1.183-2(b) as follows:

(1)   Manner in which the taxpayer carries on the activity.

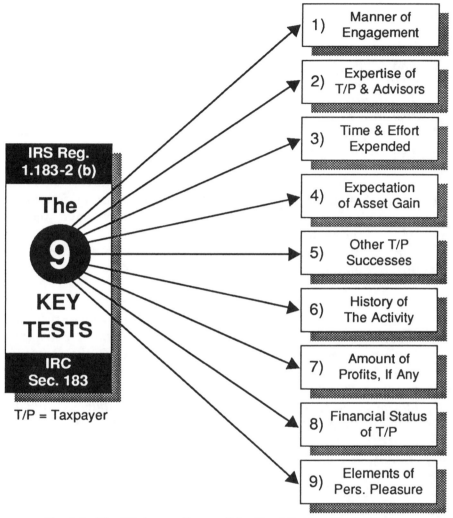

Fig. 8.1 - The "Relevant Factors" for Establishing Profit Motive

(2)   The expertise of the taxpayer or his advisors.

These two factors alone expose your inner genuineness before you yourself know it is being exposed. Are you "prequalified" in some way, or are you venturing into a new experience?

More specifically, Regulation § 1.183-2(b)(1): *Manner*, says—

*The fact that the taxpayer carries on the activity in a businesslike manner and **maintains complete and accurate books** may indicate that the activity is engaged in for profit. Similarly, where an activity is carried on in a manner **substantially similar to other activities** of the same nature **which are profitable**, a profit motive may be indicated. A change of operating methods, adoption of new techniques or abandonment of unprofitable methods in a manner consistent with an intent to improve profitability may also indicate a profit motive.*

All of which means that you have to conduct your LLC business activity as though you expected it to be profitable. If you follow the practices of other similar small businesses which have made a profit, you are on the right track.

Supplementing your manner of operation is the expertise factor. On this, Regulation § 1.183-2(b)(2): *Expertise*, says—

*Preparation for the activity by extensive study of its accepted business, economic, and scientific practices, or consultation with those who are expert therein, may indicate that the taxpayer has a profit motive where the taxpayer carries on the activity in accordance with such practices. Where a taxpayer . . . does not carry on the activity in accordance with such expert advice, a lack of intent to derive profit may be indicated unless it appears that the taxpayer is attempting to develop **new or superior techniques** which may result in profits from the activity.* [Emphasis added.]

This subregulation is telling you to prepare for your activity diligently, and follow "established practices" where they fit your situation. If you branch off into new and superior techniques, that's O.K., providing you have sought some expert advice on their feasibility. The whole idea is to demonstrate that you have the necessary savvy to run your LLC business prudently.

Time and Effort Expended

Factor (3) is captioned in Regulation § 1.183-2(b) as follows:

(3)   The time and effort expended by the taxpayer in carrying on the activity.

This particular factor is designed to assess your "devotion to duty." Its objective is to determine whether you are an active participant or a happy-go-lucky passive owner. As a passive participant, are you a wheeler-dealer goading others into taking risks with their money, while you sit on the sidelines criticizing?
   As to this factor, Regulation § 1.183-2(b)(3): *Time and effort*, specifically says—

*The fact that the taxpayer devotes much of his personal time and effort to carrying on an activity, particularly if the activity **does not have substantial personal or recreational aspects**, may indicate an intention to derive a profit. A taxpayer's withdrawal from another occupation to devote most of his energies to the activity may also be evidence that the activity is engaged in for profit. The fact that the taxpayer devotes a limited amount of time to an activity does not necessarily indicate a lack of profit motive where the taxpayer **employs competent and qualified persons** to carry on such activity.* [Emphasis added.]

The key concern of Test 3 is the amount of time and effort that you devote to the serious side of business, in contrast to the amount of tax deductions and losses that you derive from it. If your LLC business supplements in some connected way your livelihood occupation during its off-season, this will stand you well. In almost every livelihood business or occupation, there are off seasons, weekends, and spare moments that you can devote to your LLC business. Most livelihood businesses take about 200 hours (for work and commute) of an average 720-hour month. If you devote whatever off-duty time and effort you have available to your Section 183 activity, in a serious and deliberate manner, this one factor alone could signify your for-profit intentions.

Expectation & Other Successes

Factors (4) and (5) are captioned in Regulation § 1.183-2(b) as:

(4)   Expectation that assets used in the activity may appreciate in value.

(5)   The success of the taxpayer in carrying on other similar or dissimilar activities.

These two factors are designed to test your ordinary business acumen. With respect to profits made elsewhere, if any, did you make good business decisions? Did you undertake any previous business seriously, or did you do so primarily for its tax benefits? Was it a hobby, or were you cavalier about financial, tax, and accounting matters?

As to factor (4) — Test 4 — Regulation § 1.183-2(b)(4): *Expectation of appreciation*, reads as follows:

The term "profit" encompasses appreciation in the value of the assets, such as land, used in the activity. Thus, the taxpayer may intend to derive profit from the operation of the activity, and may also intend that, even if no profit from current operations is derived, an overall profit will result when appreciation in value of the land . . . is realized, since income from the activity together with the appreciation of land will exceed expenses of operation.

This test assumes that, if you use ordinary business prudence, you'll acquire appreciation-type assets (land, buildings, franchises, goodwill, licenses, etc.) at competitive market values. If the assets do appreciate in value, and you sell, you are bound to make some profit, called "capital gain." Even the someday expectation of capital gain is indicative of your profit motivation.

As to Test 5, Regulation § 1.183-2(b)(5): *Other successes,* reads in full as—

The fact that the taxpayer has engaged in similar activities in the past and converted them from unprofitable to profitable enterprises may indicate that he is engaged in the present activity for profit, even though the activity is presently unprofitable.

This test says that if you have operated a similar — or even dissimilar — business in the past, and it was profitable at some point, you probably intend to turn a profit in your current activity. In other words, your sound business judgment in the past is considered transferable to your current and future businesses.

History of Income & Losses

If you have been engaged in your current LLC business activity for a number of years before being challenged by the IRS, factor (6) — Test 6 — is a comprehensive review of your efforts therewith. This test is captioned in Regulation § 1.183-2(b) as follows—

(6)   The taxpayer's history of income or losses with respect to the activity.

The phrase "with respect to **the** activity" means the current activity only. It does not include any prior activities considered in Test 5.

Subregulation § 1.183-2(b)(6): *History of income*, reads:

*A series of losses during the initial or start-up stage of an activity may not necessarily be an indication that the activity is not engaged in for profit. However, where losses continue to be sustained **beyond the period which customarily is necessary** to bring the operation to profitable status such continued losses, if not explainable, as due to customary business risks or reverses, may be indicative that the activity is not being engaged in for profit. If losses are sustained because of **unforeseen or fortuitous circumstances** which are beyond the control of the taxpayer, such as drought, disease, fire, theft, weather damages, other involuntary conversions, or depressed market conditions, such losses would not be an indication that the activity is not engaged in for profit. A series of years in which net income was realized would of course be strong evidence that the activity is engaged in for profit.*

Test 6 is your best opportunity to explain your trials and tribulations of a long series of loss years. If, for some reason other than not-for-profit, you have suffered several consecutive loss years, you have some convincing to do.

Explaining a long series of losses is best achieved by characterizing them as three separate types or classes (as depicted in Figure 8.2). Type I losses are those occurring during your initial startup years. Type II losses are those due to unforeseen and uncontrolled events. Type III losses are those which occur after one or more consecutive profit years. If you experience Types I, II, and III losses consecutively, you'll have real difficulty explaining them!

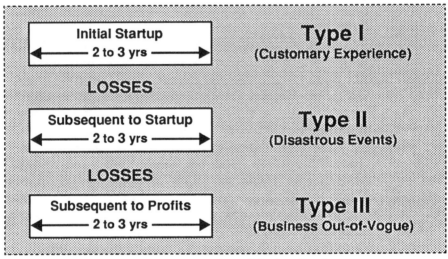

Fig. 8.2 - The "Loss Types" In Any Business

In most new business startups, it takes about three years to get into the profit-making mode. Section 183 allows only two years. Two years is a little unrealistic. Therefore, we interpret these two years as two *full* 12-month years after a part-year which is your startup year. A "part-year" is less than 12 months (obviously). It is "customary" to lose money in the first couple of years in any new business, be it an LLC or otherwise.

If **other than** during the startup years — such as Types II or III in Figure 8.2 — you have three loss years in a row, you had better have good explanations. There may have been a major fire, earthquake, or flood where your business premises are located. There may have been an airport or highway expansion project which cut off ready access to your business premises. Your product or service suddenly went out of vogue. For example, you may have been selling sports paraphernalia endorsing your home team, and the home team moves to a distant geographic area. To substantiate these facts appropriate photographs, newspaper articles, legal filings, insurance claims, police records, health and safety inspections, etc. will be most helpful.

Occasional Profits & Status

There is one basic idea behind allowing any Section 183 losses, whether startup or otherwise. There has to be a vision, some hope, some evidence of making a profit, somewhere down the line. Towards this end, occasional profits and the financial status of the taxpayer are important test considerations. This is where factors (7) and (8) come into play. These two factors/tests are captioned in Regulation § 1.183-2(b) as—

(7)   The amount of occasional profits, if any, which are earned.

(8)   The financial status of the taxpayer.

As to Test 7, Regulation § 1.183-2(b)(7): *Occasional profits*, reads as—

*The amount of profits **in relation to the amount** of losses incurred, and **in relation to the amount of the taxpayer's investment** and the value of the assets used in the activity, may provide useful criteria in determining the taxpayer's intent. An occasional small profit from an activity generating large losses, or from an activity in which the taxpayer has made a large investment, would not generally be determinative that the activity is engaged in for profit. However, **substantial profit, though only occasional**, would generally be indicative that an activity is engaged in for profit, where the investment or losses are comparatively small. Moreover, an opportunity to earn a substantial ultimate profit in **a highly speculative venture** is ordinarily sufficient to indicate . . . a for-profit activity.*

There you have it! You have got to show some profit, or real profit potential, at some time in the whole course of your venture. Never ever having a profit just won't fly.

Test 8, Regulation § 1.183-2(b)(8): *Financial status*, reads—

The fact that the taxpayer does not have substantial income or capital from sources other than the activity may indicate that an activity is engaged in for profit. Substantial income from sources other than the activity (particularly if the losses from the activity generate substantial tax benefits) may indicate that the activity is not engaged in for profit. . . .

Test 8 pretty well spotlights the nature of any not-for-profit venture. What the IRS is really targeting in Test 8 are the relative tax benefits between your LLC business and your livelihood activities. The central message is that if your LLC tax benefits are too great, you are more motivated by tax reasons than by profit reasons. This is the precursor for citing your Section 183 activity as a sham.

Elements of Personal Pleasure

The last and final relevant factor is Test 9. This test is captioned in Regulation § 1.183-2(b) as—

(9) Elements of personal pleasure or recreation.

This test is almost self-explanatory, but not fully so.

As to factor (9), § Regulation 1.183-2(b)(9): *Elements of pleasure*, reads in essential part as—

The presence of personal motives in carrying on of an activity may indicate that the activity is not engaged in for profit, especially where there are recreational or personal elements involved. On the other hand, a profit motivation may be indicated where an activity lacks any appeal other than profit. It is not, however, necessary that an activity be engaged in with the exclusive intention of deriving a profit or with the intention of maximizing profits. . . . An activity will not be treated as not engaged in for profit merely because the taxpayer has purposes or motivations other than solely to make a profit. Also, the fact that the taxpayer derives personal pleasure from engaging in the activity is not sufficient to cause the activity to be classed as not engaged in for profit if the activity is in fact engaged in for profit as evidenced by other factors. [Emphasis added.]

Test 9 is really the "wrap-up" test of the evidence that comes forth from Tests 1 through 8. In other words, the IRS considers the extent and degree of personal pleasure (such as whopping tax writeoffs) in an activity as the strongest indicator of your true motivation therewith. It is not that all personal pleasure and recreational elements (such as in business travel) are prohibited. It is that elements in any sophisticated business modeling of your LLC must be subordinated to the longer-term objective of deriving a respectable profit somewhere in the reasonable course of time.

No matter how many profit motive tests (criteria) you pass or fail, Test 9 is usually the clincher when your LLC business comes under scrutiny. This test silently permeates all others.

Buying Tax Benefits

Investing in a venture for tax reasons — that is, buying tax benefits — is not the same as investing for profit reasons. Nor is it the same as carrying on a business with economic substance in mind. When the amount of purported writeoffs in the first year exceeds the actual investment itself, we have what is classed as a *tax motivated* transaction. The true motivating factor arises from the tax benefits derived: NOT from the eventual livelihood aspects of the enterprise. As a result, said transactions are not tax recognized.

Tax motivation — in contrast to profit motivation — blinds one to the economic realities at hand. An exemplary case on point is that of *J.P. Meyers*, 92-2 USTC, ¶ 50,471. The venture was promoted as "Gold for Tax Dollars" by the International Monetary Exchange (IME), a Panamanian corporation. The offering literature "promised" a $4 tax writeoff for each $1 invested. An investor was to deposit in cash one-fourth of the amount of the tax deduction he desired.

For the case cited, taxpayer Meyers alleged that he invested $100,000 in IME for a mineral lease consisting of 250,000 cubic feet of auriferous (gold bearing) gravel in Panama. The acquisition cost of this mineral lease was $400,000 (allegedly). Of this amount, $300,000 was covered by a nonrecourse "loan" secured by the mineral claim itself. Therefore, Meyers took an immediate $400,000 writeoff. The tax deduction was based on IRC Section 616(a): *Development Expenditures*.

In court, Meyers presented no factual evidence that any development work was ever performed on his mineral leased property. He offered two invoices, each for $200,000, stating: "Paid for development work." The invoices did not describe the type or extent of development work. No reference was made whatsoever as to the existence of any amount of gold in his 250,000 cubic feet of gravel. The two paid invoices were forwarded to Meyers with a letter signed by M.M. Murphy, the principal agent for IME. The name M.M. Murphy was an alias for G.L. Rogers (real name) who used two other aliases: P.T. Smith and C.D. Blu. Testimony and documentation by the IRS showed that G.L. Rogers (the real person) was serving a 25-year prison sentence in Arizona for grand larceny when IME was formed.

When asked for backup documentation to support his $100,000 investment, Meyers offered only a photocopy of the front side of a check for $50,000. He did not produce the canceled check to show that it actually had been negotiated.

Meyers alleged that $300,000 was a loan advanced to him by IME. The IRS submitted testimony and evidence that IME was a shell corporation. It had no assets; it had no monies to loan; it had no personnel; it had no workers or miners; it had no mining equipment; it had no license to operate in Panama; it had no mining leases of any kind; it had no survey maps of the area where the mining was to take place; it had no records of geological samples being taken to appraise the commercial viability of the operation.

What puzzled the court most was why Meyers, who had a bachelor's degree in geology, never investigated the matter more intelligently. He never requested a professional assay of the auriferous gravel; he never requested a progress report on the development aspects; he never requested an accounting on his (alleged) $100,000 investment. He never inquired into the background and track record of the IME principals. He was totally blinded by the tax benefits, and he entered into the transaction solely for that reason.

Now you know why Section 183 is on the books. When there are substantial tax deductions up front, there has to be some provision for scrutinizing and testing them

Rebutting the Presumption

Section 183 is premised entirely upon a statutory presumption. The presumption is that, unless you can show a net profit in three out of five consecutive operating years, you are engaged in a tax-motivated activity which is not for profit. This is the substance of Section 183(d): *Presumption.*

We want to stress that the thesis of Section 183 is a **presumption** only. It is not some new law of economics. It is not a dictate of Congress, as the IRS would have you believe. It is not a law that rules out business recessions, business disasters, product liabilities, customer lawsuits, or plain old-fashioned bad luck in your otherwise genuine endeavors. It is a rebuttable presumption.

How do you rebut the presumption?

Answer: By corralling those facts and circumstances that establish the economic substance of your LLC endeavors. The term "economic substance" means real money on the line, real expenditures incurred, real debt assumed, and real work (physical and mental) trying to make ends meet.

Let us illustrate with a down-home example (settled out of court). The taxpayer was a real estate agent: an unmarried woman whom we'll call "Mary." Mary owned 50 head of cattle which she grazed on rental pasture land. She had been doing this for four years (all at losses) when the IRS stepped in.

The IRS auditor asserted that none of Mary's cattle losses were allowable. He wrote to Mary saying—

"From the information you have provided, the only alternative for me to conclude is that your cattle raising venture is not engaged in for profit.

Under IRS Code rules, a business must show a profit in 3 of 5 consecutive years. If you do show a profit in the coming years, you may be able to overcome the decision made at this time.

_____/s/_____

IRS Auditor"

Included with the above disallowance statement was a tax bill for $15,130 **Balance Due** . . . with penalties.

Mary prepared a 4-page typewritten protest and response. Her preamble/introductory paragraph read—

"You have erred in your interpretation and application of Code Sec. 183. You have made a *subjective inference* rather than an objective analysis of all facts and circumstances surrounding the case.

"Reg. 1.183-2(b) states quite specifically that . . . *No one factor is determinative* . . . [when] *determining whether an activity is engaged in for profit.* You have considered net operating losses only . . . and no other factors. You have not considered the many hours of backbreaking hard work that I've put in branding, feeding, calving, vaccinating, culling, carting dead carcasses, and shoveling manure for 50 head of commercial cattle and their calves. These are not house pets and they cannot be raced for sport or ridden for pleasure.

Mary then went on to cite all nine of the Figure 8.1 factors, and filled in the pertinent facts and circumstances. In reality, Mary was born and reared on a farm. She married a cattle rancher and assisted him until she was divorced. She then assisted a 70-year-old cattle ranching friend, from whom she bought the 50 head of cattle for her own enterprise.

Some six months later, Mary received an official notification from her local IRS District Director. The letter said—

We are pleased to tell you that our examination of your tax returns for the above periods show **no change is necessary in** *your reported tax* [as originally filed].

Thus you see: If you pass the scrutiny tests of Regulation § 1.183-2(b): *Relevant Factors*, you **can** be allowed your Section 183 losses. In Mary's case, this was four loss years in a row.

9

AT-RISK LIMITATIONS

> When A Partnership Or S Corporation Experiences A Net Operating Loss, A Prorata Share Of That Loss Is Passed Through To LLC Members. When Allowed, The Loss Can Be Used To Offset Other Sources Of Income On Form 1040. But, There's A Catch! Section 465 Limits The Allowable Loss To The Sum Of CASH, PROPERTY, And RECOURSE Borrowings That Each Member (Separately) Has "At Risk." Targeted As NOT AT RISK Are Those Brilliantly Layered And Circular Liability Schemes — Called "Nonrecourse Financing" — Which Are Often Pursued. For Separating The At-Risk From Not-At-Risk Amounts, Form 6198 Is Required.

One of the concerns of an LLC activity — or of any business endeavor, for that matter — is the adequacy of investment capital put on the line. In a partnership LLC, one test of this adequacy is the capital account of each partner at the end of the taxable year. If a partner has a positive ending balance, the entity can pass through to him his prorata share of operating losses.

Once an operating loss is passed through to an LLC member, another loss accounting concern arises. This time, it applies at the distributee (recipient) level, rather than at the entity level. Suppose, for example, that the entity pass-through was a $20,000 loss. Can the recipient automatically write off (deduct) the entire amount on his income tax return?

The answer: Maybe . . . or, maybe not. It depends on other loss limitation rules — there are several — in the Internal Revenue Code.

Because an LLC is a relatively new business entity form, the term "LLC" is not specifically identified in statutory wording of applicable loss laws. One such law is the at-risk rule of Section 465: *Deductions Limited to Amount at Risk*.

Section 465 applies to all activities where *nonrecourse debt* constitutes the primary source of risk. Such debt means that no one is personally liable for its repayment. In retrospect, it appears as though Section 465 had LLCs in mind. The entrepreneurial psyche that goes with loading a business with nonrecourse debt is the same psyche associated with limited liability motivation. The drive is to make large profits — or large losses — with other people's money.

Accordingly, in this chapter we want to introduce Section 465 to you; touch on its highlights, and explain it in a way that makes good economic sense. We also want to stress certain points to tuck away in your memory bank as you pursue your LLC goals. This at-risk rule could be the single, most important loss limitation feature that you'll encounter when preparing your own Form 1040 return.

Where on Form 1040?

You've probably missed it in the past. But it's there on one of the schedules that you attach to Form 1040: *U.S. Individual Income Tax Return*. As a distributee/recipient of a pass-through entity, you'll receive an "information return" from either a partnership or an S corporation. If you're an LLC member of a partnership, you'll receive *Schedule K-1 (Form 1065)*; if an LLC of an S corporation, you'll receive *Schedule K-1 (Form 1120S)*. The "1065" is: Return of Partnership Income; the "1120S" is: Return for an S corporation. Partnerships and S corporations have nearly identical pass-through provisions.

On either of these Schedules K-1, you are instructed as to what information to report on your Form 1040. One particular schedule for attaching to your 1040 is **Part II** of Schedule E: *Income or Loss from Partnerships and S Corporations*. As a current or potential LLC member, we urge that you procure a copy of Schedule E (Form 1040), Part II, for your own instructional reference. In the meantime, the information in Figure 9.1 can be helpful. Note the shaded portion: "Investment at Risk?"

Sched. E (1040)	SUPPLEMENTAL INCOME AND LOSS			Year	
Part II	**Income or Loss From Partnerships & S Corporations**				
Headnote re Form 6198. See Text.				**Investment at Risk?**	
(a) Name	(b) P or S	(b) Foreign	(b) Tax ID	(e) All	(f) Some
[Continued in Figure 10.1]					

Fig. 9.1 - Upper Portion of Part II of Schedule E (Form 1040)

A small-print instruction just below the Part II caption reads:

*If you report a loss from an at-risk activity, you **must** check either column (e) or (f) to describe your investment in that activity.*

Investment at Risk?
Col. (e) All is at risk ☐
Col. (f) Some is not at risk ☐

See instructions.

The instructions tell you to file **Form 6198** if you checked the Col. (f) box. That form is titled: *At Risk Limitations*. We'll come back to this form later.

The instructions also tell you that—

The at-risk rules generally limit the amount of loss (including loss on the disposition of assets) you can claim to the amount you could actually lose in the activity.

Now, back to that $20,000 hypothetical pass-through loss, mentioned above. Suppose your actual real money on the line is

$5,000. Even though the LLC entity said that your distributive share of its operational loss was $20,000, the maximum loss that you can deduct for that year is $5,000. The unused loss of $15,000 can be carried over to subsequent years, provided that your at-risk amounts for each carryover year are greater than zero. Such is the substance of Section 465.

Introductory Statutory Wording

Section 465: *Deductions Limited to Amount at Risk*, consists of approximately 3,600 words. It is arranged into five subsections, as follows:

(a)	Limitation to Amount at Risk	(~ 170 words)
(b)	Amounts Considered at Risk	(~ 1,000 words)
(c)	Activities to which Section Applies	(~ 2,300 words)
(d)	Definition of Loss	(~ 70 words)
(e)	Recapture of Losses where Amount at Risk is Less than Zero	(~ 110 words)

Paragraph (1) of subsection (a) reads principally as—

In the case of an individual . . . engaged in an activity to which this section applies, any loss from such activity for the taxable year shall be allowed only to the extent . . . to which the taxpayer is at risk . . . for such activity at the close of the taxable year.

Note two particular terms in this citation: "an individual" and "such activity." An individual is a distributee/recipient of a pass-through entity of any form. Common such entities are estates, trusts, partnerships, S corporations, PHCs (personal holding companies), PSCs (personal service corporations), LLCs, and closely-held C corporations. A "closely-held" C corporation is an entity arrangement consisting of five or fewer individuals owning 50% or more of the corporate stock. The obvious reason for including closely-held C-type entities is to dissuade the principals from sheltering large taxable income sources with creative paper losses convertible to large deductions.

The term "such activity" pointed out above has an implication of its own. If the pass-through entity engages in two or more functionally separate activities — which it can do — the loss for each activity (for each taxable year) has to be separately identified. This is because each functionally separate activity is an accounting center of its own. Each such center carries its own benefits and burdens, including the at-risk limitation rules. We need to explain the requirement for per activity accounting.

Why Deductions "Per Activity"

Paragraphs (1) and (3) of subsection (c): *Activities to which Section Applies*, end with the clause—

shall be treated as a separate activity.

The activities listed in subsection (c) are any—

1. film or video tape,
2. equipment leased or held for leasing,
3. farm or farming operation,
4. oil and gas property,
5. geothermal property,
6. trade or business,
7. rental real estate, and
8. activities not above described.

An "activity" is a specific pursuit for achieving an end of its own. It is not normally thought of as an ongoing trade or business or as an indefinite means of producing income. An activity for at-risk tax purposes is analogous to an experimental or developmental "project." Some grand idea is being trialed-and-errored. If the result desired does not work out, the project is abandoned. If the results are promising, new enterprises are formed. Special deduction allowances and tax credits are afforded to such activities. These tax benefits attract high risk-taking entrepreneurs who, with clever financing schemes, often get by with minimal money out of their own personal pockets.

By separating each activity/project from all others, each becomes an "accounting center" of its own. As such, the allowable deductions therewith can be better definitized. Characteristically, these projects inherently produce losses . . . often large losses. The purpose of Section 465 is to limit the deductibility of such losses. It is easier to identify and track these losses, activity-by-activity, than by aggregating them.

Nevertheless, aggregation rules do apply to certain partnerships and S corporations (and, of course, to qualified C corporations). The "certain" is spelled out in subsection 465(c)(3)(B): *Aggregation of Activities where Taxpayer Actively Participates in Management of Trade or Business.* This subsection reads in pertinent part—

> *Activities . . . which constitute a trade or business shall be treated as one activity if—*
>> *(i) the taxpayer actively participates in the management of such trade or business or*
>> *(ii) such trade or business is carried on by a partnership or S corporation and 65% or more of the losses for the taxable year is allocable to persons who actively participate in the management of the trade or business.*

This aggregation rule appears to particularly accommodate a bona fide LLC business. Subparagraph (i) applies to single member LLCs, whereas subparagraph (ii) applies to LLC partnerships and to S corporation LLCs (if so elected). By definition, an LLC person is an owner-manager, as well as an investor, in the business in which he or she actively participates. This is why Figure 9.1 asks for the name of the LLC entity as a whole, rather than requiring the separate identification of each at-risk activity.

Meaning of "Amount at Risk"

It sounds like a no-brainer. What does "amount at risk" mean? For tax purposes, it means the actual amount of financial loss that one can suffer in a business-motivated activity that can go sour. Statutorily, said amount is defined by Section 465(b): *Amounts*

Considered at Risk. The term "amounts" (plural) means the sum of several risk items.

We paraphrase Section 465(b) as follows:

A taxpayer shall be considered at risk for an activity with respect to amounts that include—

1. *the amount of money contributed to the activity,*

2. *the adjusted basis of other property contributed to the activity, and*

3. *amounts borrowed for use in the activity to the extent that the taxpayer is **personally liable for its repayment**.* [Emphasis added.]

We capstone these three items for you in Figure 9.2. We also make references to other applicable paragraphs in Section 465. Figure 9.2 represents the core of the at-risk limitation computations which are disclosed on Form 6198.

The requirement that a taxpayer be personally liable for the repayment of borrowed money strikes at the heart of the LLC concept. Obviously, one is not at risk when protected in any limited liability way. Subsection 465(b)(4) makes this point clear:

A taxpayer shall not be considered at risk with respect to amounts protected against loss through nonrecourse financing, guarantees, stop loss agreements, or other similar arrangements.

Of the three types of at-risk amounts above (cash, property, and borrowed money), the use of borrowed money is the most at-risk contentious . . . and the most litigated. For resolving such issues, the U.S. Tax Court applies the test of **ultimate liability**. The court seeks to distinguish persons who are personally liable from those who are merely guarantors or are, in some way, only secondarily liable for the repayment of borrowed amounts. The ultimately liable person is the party of last recourse. Such person is one whose

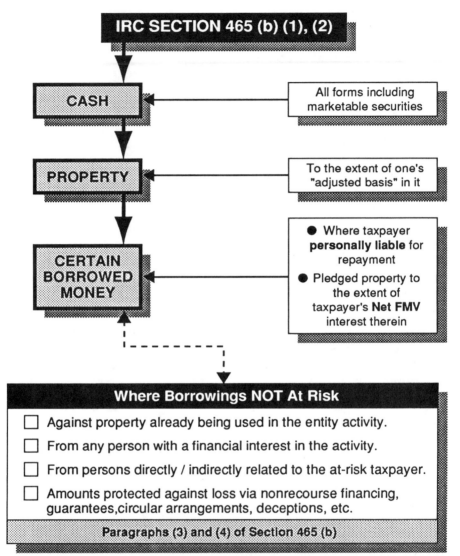

Fig. 9.2 - Core Items Readily Considered At Risk

funds stand as the final source of repayment should other sources fail to satisfy the obligation.

A landmark case on point is that of *M.W Melvin*, CA-9, 90-1 USTC ¶ 50,052. Taxpayer Melvin was one of 73 limited partners who pledged (prorata) "deferred capital contributions" as collateral for a $3,500,000 (3.5 million) recourse bank loan. Under this arrangement, Melvin's prorata share was 0.6232% or $21,812. The activity in which the borrowed money was used incurred a net operating loss of $12,515,318 (12.5 million). Accordingly, the taxpayer claimed a deductible loss of $78,000 ($12,515,318 x 0.006232) on the joint return with his wife. The IRS disallowed the $78,000 but did allow the $21,812. The taxpayer appealed to the U.S. Court of Appeals for the Ninth Circuit (CA-9) in California.

The Appeals Court affirmed the Tax Court's opinion in that—

Melvin was not at risk for amounts exceeding his prorata share of his partnership's $3,500,000 bank loan. Section 465(b)(4) excludes deductions for risks that are protected by "loss-limiting arrangements." The court deemed Melvin to be protected against loss by a right of reimbursement (under California law) from the other limited partners to the extent of their deferred capital contribution.

Finessing of Financing

We want to emphasize the above points with respect to borrowed money for use in an LLC activity. Virtually every activity of substance seeking a profit depends on the use of borrowed money. And human nature is such that the instigating entrepreneurs insist on using other people's money rather than their own. The LLC psyche, with its tunnel focus on the "LL", makes LLCs particularly vulnerable to those financing arrangements where direct personal liability is nil. The consequence is the use of unsecured promissory notes, encumbered property for collateral, personal handshakes, "part of the action" if the business succeeds, and other intangible and unenforceable security arrangements. Brilliance, sophistication, and deception are the hallmarks of these financial schemes. The IRS calls these: *nonrecourse financing*. We call them "finessing financing."

Let us illustrate.

In the *Melvin* 9th Circuit Appeals Court case above, the loss by the partnership for the taxable year was just over $12,500,000. Of this amount, we know that $3,500,000 was covered by a recourse bank loan. This left $9,000,000 — 9 million dollars — that was financed finessingly. How was this done?

Answer: We don't know exactly. The *Melvin* court did not address this specific issue. We do have some thoughts on the matter. We know that some unsuspecting group of unrelated creditors lost $9 million.

Finessing financing has three general characteristics, namely:

(1) Chain of obligors,
(2) Obfuscating (and circular wording),
(3) Ambiguous legal references

All of these arrangements end with an open-ended enforceability clause that—

> This instrument is executed and intended to be performed in the state of _____, and the laws of that state shall govern its interpretation and effect.

This means that a creditor has to get an attorney to find out what his enforceability rights are. Meanwhile, the creditor proceeds on good faith in his own interpretation of what the wording means.

A nonrecourse financing arrangement goes something like this. In exchange for money or marketable securities, a cooperative lender (usually some friend or associate) is given an official-looking document (on high-grade embossed paper) with conspicuously displayed seals, stamps, and signatures. The document is bold-print captioned: PROMISSORY NOTE. On its face, the note indicates the amount borrowed, the rate of interest to be paid (by the obligor(s)), and the due date for full payment. Prefatory wording to the particulars of the note indicate that it is either collateralized, guaranteed, warranted, pledged, accredited, licensed, insured, or some other term implying securitization in some manner.

Often the "security" is some microfractional interest — such as 0.012973 percent — in a high-sounding business operation (located out of state), or in some parcel of realty in a wilderness area or open space preserve, or in items of high-tech equipment and merchandise in a bonded warehouse, or in "proven reserves" in an offshore haven. With such a stream of clever and emotionally appealing wording, even the most cynical lender feels confident that he will get his money back. The first indication that he won't (get his money back) is when the using activity files for bankruptcy. Or, if the borrowing entity wishes to continue doing business, it engages a credit managing service to prepare a Workout Agreement for pennies on the dollar. The Workout Agreement legally describes the amount loaned as an "Unsecured Claim."

And so it goes. The borrowing entity principals, managers, and members are "off the hook." They are not personally liable. Still, they want a tax deduction (prorata) for the money they allegedly borrowed but never had to pay back. In the *Melvin* case above, a total of $9,000,000 disappeared via 73 (mostly worthless) I.O.U.s.

Example of "Circular" Financing

We never cease to be amazed by the deceptive brilliance of some entrepreneurs when structuring their financial transactions. It's scary. It is scary because some LLC enthusiasts will want to raise the finessing bar even higher. A good example of what we are getting at is the case of *R.L. Whitmire*, CA-9; 99-1 USTC ¶ 50,563. This is a published case consisting of over 4,000 words of citable judicial inquiry and rationalization. The appeals court itself marveled at the artful structuring of so many layers of protection that precluded any realistic possibility of Whitmire ever being held personally responsible for the repaying of borrowed funds.

Whitmire executed a Subscription Agreement with Petunia, et al, in exchange for a limited partnership interest. He contributed $25,031.50 ($16,281.50 in cash and a recourse promissory note for $8,750) in a double, triple-leaseback computer equipment arrangement. Whitmire also subscribed to his being personally liable under a Petunia-Venture Note for an amount up to 434.75% of his capital contribution. This meant (to Whitmire) that his potential tax deduction could be $108,824.45 ($25,031.50 x 4.3475) for an out-of-pocket cash amount of $16,281.50. If allowed, his deduction would be 6.6837 times his true economic risk.

Editorial Note: The first indicator of a sophisticated scam is the absence of simple round numbers. Trying to mentally absorb and track odd-dollar amounts and uneven fractions and percentages catapults the reader into an early-on state of confusion.

The best that we can figure out is that the double, triple-leaseback arrangement worked like this. Alanthus Computer Corporation (ACC) was the creator of the Petunia-Venture limited partnership. ACC purchased several hundred million dollars of computer equipment from IBM (International Business Machines Corporation). ACC then leased the equipment to Manufacturers Traders Trust Company (MTT). ACC then sold the equipment *and* the lease to the Alanthus Corporation. Alanthus paid for the equipment with a recourse loan from Manufacturers Hanover Leasing Corporation (MHLC) which was secured by the equipment. Alanthus entered into a security agreement with MHLC which stated that MTT would make the lease payments directly to MHLC in satisfaction of the loan. Alanthus would become personally liable if MTT defaulted. This was the first triple-leaseback phase.

Alanthus resold the computer equipment to F/S Computer Corporation, and F/S executed an agreement by which F/S assumed all of Alanthus's rights under the MTT lease. In exchange, F/S also assumed all of Alanthus's obligations under the MHLC loan and agreement. On the same day, F/S sold the equipment and assigned the lease to F.S. Venture, subject to MHLC's and MTT's interests in the equipment. Venture immediately resold the computer equipment and assigned the lease to Petunia. In payment therefor, Petunia gave Venture a Limited Recourse Installment Promissory Note — the "Petunia-Venture Note" — whereby all Petunia partners (including Whitmire) were severally and personally liable for each of the installments of principal.

Now you have all of the classic earmarks of an outright scam.

The appeals court should have summarily thrown the case out. Instead, it painstakingly cited SIX separate layers of default that would have had to occur, before Whitmire became personally liable.

Among its concluding remarks, the court said—

In his attempt to remain entitled to deduction for "at risk" amounts, yet simultaneously limit his risk, Whitmire crossed the line by shrouding himself in too much protection to leave any "realistic possibility" that he would suffer a loss. . . . Therefore, we affirm the order of the tax court, and hold that Whitmire is not "as risk" within the meaning of section 465(b).

Now to Form 6198

Lest some LLC enthusiast is thinking of trying to outsmart Whitmire above, here's a fact you should know. Whitmire entered into his limited partnership arrangement in June, 1980. The matter was not finalized until May, 1999. That's **19 years** of entanglement with the IRS, Tax Court, and Appeals Court. Though he claimed nearly $120,000 in tax deductions over the first three years, he wound up being at risk for only his initial investment of $25,000. His deficiency assessments, penalties, interest, and attorney fees approached $250,000. Whitmire could have saved himself much aggravation had he used IRS Form 6198: *At-Risk Limitations*.

Form 6198 is one page accompanied by eight pages of instructions (about 3,500 words). The form consists of 25 entry lines, arranged in four parts as follows:

Part I — Current Year Profit (Loss) from the Activity, Including Prior Year Nondeductible Amounts

Part II — Simplified Computation of Amount at Risk

Part III — Detailed Computation of Amount at Risk

Part IV — Deductible Loss

The instructions accompanying Form 6198, though detailed, are quite straightforward. As a result, there are two categories of instruction: [1] Taxpayers other than partners or S corporation shareholders, and [2] Partners and S corporation shareholders. For LLC persons, instructions [2] are the primary focus.

The instructions at: *Amounts not at Risk*, introduce a new matter. They say—

*However, you are considered at risk for **qualified nonrecourse financing** secured by real property used in the activity of holding real property (other than mineral property). . . . [Such] financing is that for which no one is personally liable for repayment . . . [because it is] loaned or guaranteed by a Federal, state, or local government, or borrowed by you from a qualified . . . bank, savings and loan, or other person who is actively and regularly engaged in the business of lending money.*

In other words, bona fide mortgage debt on real property used in an LLC activity is considered an at-risk item. It affects one's adjusted basis in the entity activity. The allowing of qualified nonrecourse financing was tax effective on an after August 4, 1998.

Use Part II: Simplified Computation

The instructions to Part I of Form 6198 are really quite self-explanatory. As an example, the instructions to line 1 read—

Partners and S corporation shareholders. Enter the amount from line 1 of your current year Schedule K-1 (Form 1065 or Form 1120S) . . . plus any prior year loss from Schedule K-1, that you could not deduct because of the at-risk rules.

Thus, you are told not only what schedule and line number to use, but you are also reminded to include any unallowable loss from the preceding year [Sec. 465(a)(2): Deduction in Succeeding Year]. Part I ends on line 5 with the current year profit or loss from the activity. If there is a profit at this point, you do not have to complete the rest of the form.

But if there is a loss on line 5 of Part I, you need to use Part II of Form 6198 to determine how much of the loss is deductible. For an overview of what is involved in Part II, we present Figure 9.3.

Part II starts off with line 6 which is captioned—

Adjusted basis . . . in your interest in the activity.

We made quite a point of "adjusted basis" back in Chapter 7: Partnership LLC Rules. If you are a conscientious LLC person, you want to keep track of the adjusted basis in your ownership interest in the LLC entity at all times. As you'll glean from the Form 6198 instructions, Part II is designed for persons like you.

We want to call to your attention in Figure 9.3 the two boxes labeled: "Increases in Basis" and "Decreases in Basis." The items listed in the respective boxes are abbreviations of information in the instructions. Obviously, to the adjusted basis of your ownership

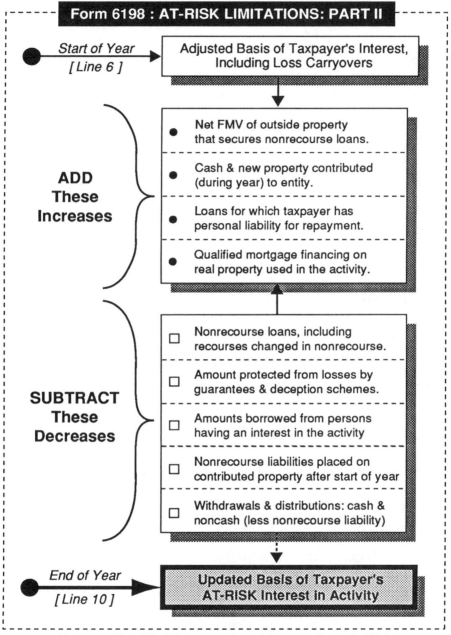

Form 6198 : AT-RISK LIMITATIONS: PART II

Start of Year
[Line 6]

Adjusted Basis of Taxpayer's Interest,
Including Loss Carryovers

**ADD
These
Increases**

- Net FMV of outside property that secures nonrecourse loans.
- Cash & new property contributed (during year) to entity.
- Loans for which taxpayer has personal liability for repayment.
- Qualified mortgage financing on real property used in the activity.

**SUBTRACT
These
Decreases**

- Nonrecourse loans, including recourses changed in nonrecourse.
- Amount protected from losses by guarantees & deception schemes.
- Amounts borrowed from persons having an interest in the activity
- Nonrecourse liabilities placed on contributed property after start of year
- Withdrawals & distributions: cash & noncash (less nonrecourse liability)

End of Year
[Line 10]

**Updated Basis of Taxpayer's
AT-RISK Interest in Activity**

Fig. 9.3 - Simplified Computation of Amount Truly At Risk

interest at the beginning of the tax year, you add your increases in basis, then subtract your decreases in basis (for the same tax year). At the end of the year, you have an updated adjusted basis. This updated — or end of year — basis may be:

(i)   more than zero (a positive amount)
(ii)   zero
(iii) less than zero (a negative amount)

Whatever this end-of-year basis amount is, it is designated as line 10 in Part II of Form 6198. [Note this in Figure 9.3.]

At line 10, and from line 10 on, there are small-print instructions (right on the form) that tell you what to do next.

If line 10 is more than zero (basis "i" above), you are told to—

*Enter the **smaller of line 5** [adjusted basis start of year] or line 10 [adjusted basis end of year]. . . as a deductible loss on your tax return.*

Examples. Suppose that line 5 is $4,000 and line 10 is $10,000. The "smaller of" the two is your deductible loss. That is, your deductible loss is $4,000 and your at-risk basis in the entity is reduced to $6,000. Now, suppose that line 5 is $17,000 and line 10 remains at $10,000. The "smaller of" the two is $10,000. Your basis is reduced to zero. So, you have an unallowed loss of $7,000 which can be carried over to the next succeeding taxable year.

If the adjusted basis of your LLC interests at the end of the year is zero (basis "ii" above), you get no at-risk deduction loss whatsoever. Your prorata share of the entity's operating loss is carried over (in full) to the following year.

If, on the other hand, your ending adjusted basis is *less than* zero (basis "iii" above) — say, <$5,000> — what happens? Answer: This is what is called: *at-risk loss* **recapture**. That is, you "recapture" the <$5,000> by entering it as a positive amount on the very last income line (captioned: *Other income*) on page 1 of your Form 1040. This is so prescribed by Section 465(e): ***Recapture of Losses where Amount at Risk Is Less than Zero***.

10

MATERIAL PARTICIPATION

There Are 7 "Tests" For Determining Material Participation In A Trade Or Business. Meeting Any One Of The Tests Qualifies An LLC Person, Whether In A Partnership Or Proprietorship. The "Guiding Star" Is Devoting 500 Or More Hours To A Single Activity During The Year. The Purpose Of The Tests Is To Distinguish Between PASSIVE And NONPASSIVE Activities For The Allowability Of Operating Losses. For Rental Real Estate, "Active Participation" Triggers An Additional Loss Allowance. Being A "Real Estate Professional" With 750 Hours' Participation Converts A Passive Loss To Nonpassive, For Better Tax Benefits.

There is one issue that tends to be skipped over by LLC enthusiasts. The issue is: *material participation.* How much time, effort, and personal service does an LLC person devote to the activities of his company? Recall that the letter "C" in LLC means "company." The term "company" implies doing business in some for-profit form. Doing business for profit also means incurring operational losses.

So, why is the issue of material participation important to LLC persons?

Answer: The allowability of operating losses to LLC persons (as taxpayers) depends on the materiality of each person's participation in company activities. Whether in a partnership or not, an LLC person is treated by the IRS as a limited partner. That is, not only is his financial risk limited to the amount of his investment, his participation — lacking other information — is treated as nil or passive. As a passive participant, the deductibility of his share of operating losses is limited. This brings into play an entirely different loss limitation rule from that described in the preceding chapter. But, before presenting the additional limitation rule, we need to address the matter of "material participation."

The IRS treats an LLC person as having a split-tax personality. On one hand, he is considered a passive participant like that of a limited partner. On the other hand, he actively participates in the management and working of the LLC activity, like that of a general partner. Thus, an LLC person is a "participant" to one degree or another. This is because he has a direct ownership interest in the operational affairs of the business.

There are three classes of participation: passive, active, and material. The IRS and the Tax Code have prescribed certain definitions and tests for ascertaining the degree of participation in any business activity. Accordingly, in this chapter, we want to present these definitions and tests to you, point out the anomalies and exceptions, and explain the loss distinctions that occur. Most helpful in this regard are the instructions prepared by the IRS to Schedule K-1 (1065). Form 1065, recall, is titled: *Return of Partnership Income.*

Proprietorship LLCs

As we explained back in Chapter 7, a single member LLC is default classified as a proprietorship. As such, an LLC person would file Schedule C (Form 1040) or Schedule F (Form 1040) as appropriate. Schedule C, recall, is titled *Profit or Loss from Business*, whereas Schedule F is titled: *Profit or Loss from Farming.* Do note that the word "Loss" is included in these titles.

On both schedules, C and F, the material participation question and instructions are the same. In the head portion of each schedule, the question is asked—

Did you "materially participate" in the operation of this business during _____ ? ☐ *Yes,* ☐ *No. If "No", see instructions for limit on losses.*

The blank space in the question refers to the taxable year preprinted on the official form. Thus, the same question is asked year after year. One can materially participate in one year, and not materially participate in one or more subsequent years.

The instructions to Schedules C and F define "participation" this way:

*Participation . . . generally includes any work you did in connection with an activity **if you owned an interest in the activity at the time you did the work**. The capacity in which you did the work does not matter. However, work is not treated as participation if it is not work that an owner would customarily do in the same type of activity, and one of your main reasons for doing the work was to avoid the disallowance of losses or credits from the activity under the passive activity rules. [Emphasis added.]*

In other words, work performed in the activity must be genuine, and must relate to the daily and ongoing needs of the business. Make-work won't do. Especially if your only reason for doing so is to answer "Yes" to the question rather than "No". If you make a profit rather than a loss (at the end of the year), the question may be irrelevant. But you still have to answer it, nevertheless.

The instructions go on to say—

*Participation by your spouse during the tax year in an activity you own **can be counted as your participation** in the activity. This applies even if your spouse did not own an interest in the activity and whether or not you and your spouse file a joint return. [Emphasis added.]*

The instructions then list and describe SEVEN tests for determining whether you materially participate. The preface to these tests eliminates any work done as a pure investor. The studying and reviewing of financial statements, operational reports, balance sheets, etc. is regarded as nonmanagerial activity which, therefore, does not qualify as participation.

The concluding material participation instructions say, in brief—

*If you **do not** meet any of the above tests, check the "No" box. This business is a **passive activity**. If you have a loss from this business, . . . you may have to use Form 8582 [Passive Activity Loss Limitations] to figure your allowable loss. . . . Generally, you can deduct losses from passive activities only to the extent of income from passive activities.*

Partnership LLCs

In the case of a partnership LLC, the material participation question is not so directly asked, as it is for proprietorship LLCs. Nor are the partnership instructions as straightforward. The puzzle starts when an LLC person receives from the partnership an information return. Said return is Schedule K-1 (Form 1065): **Partner's Share of Income, Credits, Deductions, etc.** In the head portion of this schedule, there are 10 questions with checkboxes and entry spaces. **None** asks the question: "Did you materially participate . . .?".

The only possible hint you get is the statement which reads—

This partner is a ☐ general partner, ☐ limited partner, or ☐ limited liability company member [LLC].

Ordinarily, a general partner is considered to be an active participant in the partnership's day-to-day business activities. If he isn't active, he would be regarded as an investor. In contrast, a limited partner is considered to be a passive participant. Such a partner can actively participate, but he requires credible proof of doing so. Where does this leave an LLC person?

Answer: As an LLC person, you have to read portions of the official instructions that accompany Schedule K-1. Early on, one instruction says—

The amount of loss and deduction that you may claim on your tax return may be less than the amount reported on Schedule K-1. It is the partner's responsibility to consider and apply any applicable limitations. See Limitations on Losses, Deductions, and Credits for more information.

When you read these referenced instructions, you'll find that partnership participation is characterized either as **Passive** or **Nonpassive**. The basic distinction between the two is the extent of a partner's personal participation in the partnership activities. An interpretation complication arises because, in a partnership, rental real estate activities often constitute a dominant source of income or loss. This creates a new participation category described as: *Active participation in a rental real estate activity*. We'll comment on this participation category a little later.

Meanwhile, the K-1 instructions on material participation say—

You must determine if you materially participated (a) in each trade or business activity held through the partnership, and (b) if you were a real estate professional, in each real estate activity held through the partnership. All determinations of material participation are made based on your participation during the partnership's tax year.

In other words, the partnership accountant has no obligation to track and inform you of your participative extent. You have to do this — and prove it — on your own. You can do so by any reasonable means. This includes keeping a log of the services you performed over a period of time, the contacts you made, any travel for partnership business, and the approximate hours and places therewith. Appointment books, calendars, invoices, diaries, narrative summaries, and other evidentiary material may be used. As an LLC person, you are a part owner of the partnership and its activities. As such, you are not required to produce a time clock on every work move you make. But you are expected to demonstrate comprehension of the material participation rules.

Sources of Income or Loss

As an LLC partner, one of the first ways to demonstrate comprehension of the participation rules is by a reading of Schedule K-1 instructions. Particularly those portions that address the sources of income or loss. There are seven such sources, namely:

1. Ordinary **income (loss)** from trade or business activities
2. *Income (loss)* from rental real estate activities
3. *Income (loss)* from other rental activities
4. Portfolio *income (loss)*
5. Guaranteed payments to partners
6. Section 1231 *gain (loss)*
7. Other *income (loss)* [attach statement]

Of these seven sources of partnership income (loss), sources 1 and 2 are the most sensitive with respect to participative vs. nonparticipative decisions. Separate instructions are directed at each item. Nonparticipative effort is designated as *Passive*, whereas participative effort is designated as *Nonpassive*. When in doubt, or when having no records that document your participation, you are expected to classify any income or loss as passive.

Sources 3 and 4 are passive; source 5 is nonpassive. The instructions tell you so.

Source 6 refers to the capital gain, ordinary loss rule of Section 1231 when selling or exchanging property used in a trade or business (re Source 1) or for the production of income (re Source 2). Source 6 is the transactional accounting for one or more separate events. It is not the gain or loss from day-to-day participation. Its character as passive or nonpassive depends on how the property was used in Sources 1 or 2. Similarly, for Source 7: refunds, discounts, recapture of prior tax benefits, casualties and thefts, and qualified small business stock. Source 7 may be passive or nonpassive, depending on how the income or loss source has its origin in Sources 1 or 2.

The instructions for Sources 1 and 2 direct you to Schedule E (Form 1040), Part II thereof. The Part II is subheaded: *Income or Loss from Partnerships*, etc. We displayed the top portion of Part II back in Figure 9.1 (on page 9-3). We now display the lower portion in Figure 10.1. Without the help of this display, the characterization of passive and/or nonpassive can become confusing. Even with Figure 10.1, instructional confusion can arise. To help straighten things out, we urge that you think as follows:

PASSIVE = NONPARTICIPATIVE

[Continued from Figure 9.1]

	PASSIVE INCOME & LOSS		NONPASSIVE INCOME & LOSS		
	(g) Loss	(h) Income	(i) Loss	(j) Sec.179	(k) Income
A					
B					
C					
D					
E					

Follow instructions on form for subtotaling, etc.

Fig. 10.1 - Lower Portion of Part II of Schedule E (Form 1040)

NONPASSIVE = PARTICIPATIVE

Source 1: Trade or Business

What we have designated as "Source 1" above is actually line 1 on Schedule K-1 (Form 1065). The line 1 caption is:

Ordinary income (loss) from trade or business activities.

> **Editorial Note**: The term "trade or business" goes back to the early history of this Nation (pre 1900). At that time, there were two broad classes of livelihood: import-export *trade*, and farming-manufacturing *business*. There was very little passive activity that generated one's livelihood in those days.

Note the plural: activi**ties**, in the line 1 caption above. Thus, your LLC partnership could engage in one, two, or three separate trade or business activities. You, yourself, could participate materially in one such activity and be passive in all others. **You** have to make this distinction from your own records. The amount of income or loss reported to you on line 1 is your prorata share of the aggregate of all trade or business activities of the partnership.

With the above as background, the K-1 instructions to line 1 (Source 1) read—

> *The amount reported on line 1 is your share of the ordinary income (loss) from the trade or business activities of the partnership. Generally, where you report this amount on Form 1040 depends on whether the amount is a passive activity to you. If you are individual, find your situation below and report as instructed. (1) Report line 1 income (loss) in which you materially participated on Schedule E (Form 1040), Part II, column (i) or (k). (2) Report line 1 income (loss) in which you did not materially participate on Schedule E (Form 1040), Part II, column (g) or (h).*

A glance at Figure 10.1 reveals that columns (g) and (h) are designated as: PASSIVE *Income and Loss*, whereas columns (i) and (k) are: NONPASSIVE *Income and Loss*. While glancing, note column (j). This is a special deduction allowance for certain depreciable property used in a trade or business. If column (j) applies to you, it will be reported to you on line 9 (*Section 179 expense deductions*) of your K-1.

Material Participation: Test 1

In the K-1 instructions, there's a bold-lettered section captioned: *Material participation*. Thereunder are listed seven tests for determining whether a partner is a material participant or not. Because of the specificity and simplicity of Test 1, we regard it as the guiding star for all other tests. Nevertheless, in abbreviated form (in some cases, highly abbreviated), we display all seven tests in Figure 10.2. We'll group Tests 2 through 7 together and comment on them later.

All seven tests are listed in the K-1 instructions under the subcaption: *Individuals (other than limited partners)*. The introductory wording to the seven tests reads—

> *If you are an individual (either a general partner or a limited partner who owned a general partnership interest at all times*

during the tax year), you materially participated in an activity **only if one** *or more of the following apply.* [Emphasis added.]

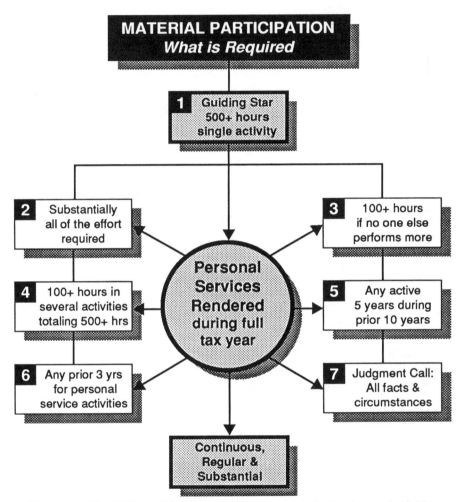

Fig. 10.2 - The "7 Tests" for Material Participation in Business Activities

The parenthesized wording above is a clear indication to us that the IRS considers an LLC person to be: "a limited partner with the ownership interests of a general partner." As such, qualifying under Test 1 is the premier goal to pursue. We call it: *The 500+ hours test.* This is your "guiding star," as Figure 10.2 indicates

The official wording of Test 1 in the K-1 instructions says that, if you are an individual, you materially participated in a trade or business activity . . . if—

1. *you participated in the activity for more than 500 hours during the tax year.*

A 500^+ hour period is about 25% of a full work year. An ordinary work year consists of 2,000 hours [8 hours/day x 5 days/week x 50 weeks (2 weeks off for vacation)]. True, you could work 10 hours/day, 6 days/week (which totals 3,000 hours per year). But if you claim more than 2,000 hours of work in a given year, you had better document your time convincingly.

Keeping track of hours worked is certainly a simple way to establish participative qualification. At 500^+ hours per activity, one could readily participate in two or three separate activities in a tax year. Suppose you qualified as materially participating in three separate trade or business activities (Source 1). Keep in mind that the Source 1 information reported to you on line 1 of Schedule K-1 (1065) is the aggregate *net* income (loss) from all Source 1 activities of the partnership. This being the case, how would you allocate a K-1 reported amount of $5,000 (a positive number)?

Answer: As we illustrate comprehensively below. To add instructional interest to our hypothetical example, consider that the partnership has five separate Source 1 activities: A, B, C, D, and E. Two make a profit and three make a loss. You wouldn't know this from the $5,000 aggregate amount reported to you on line 1 of your K-1. Now what?

Hypothetical Allocation Example

Knowing that you worked in three Source 1 activities for the year, and learning the partnership had two more of such activities, what is the first thing you do?

You turn to page 2 of the Schedule K-1 prepared for you by the partnership, and examine line 25. This is the very last line on the official form. It is captioned:

Supplemental information required to be reported separately by each partner.

If there is no entry there (seven full-page-width blank lines), contact the partnership accountant. Request/insist that he provide you with the partnership's allocation of the $5,000 among its five Source 1 activities.

After persistent requests, suppose the partnership provided you with the following data—

Activity	"A" —	3,000	}	
"	"B" —	<2,000>	}	Aggregate
"	"C" —	<1,000>	}	net total $5,000
"	"D" —	<1,000>	}	(positive amount)
"	"E" —	6,000	}	

Suppose you can identify with activities "A", "B", and "D" as having materially participated in each. How do you report on your Schedule E (1040), Part II?

Answer: What you cannot establish as a material participation activity, you default to the **Passive** income and loss category. Thus, "C" and "E" become passive activities for you. Accordingly, you enter as follows [refer to Figure 10.1, if you like]:

Col. (g)	:	Activity "C",	$1,000 *passive* loss
Col. (h)	:	Activity "E",	6,000 *passive* income
Col. (i)	:	Activity "B",	2,000 *nonpassive* loss
Col. (i)	:	Activity "D",	1,000 *nonpassive* loss
Col. (k)	:	Activity "A",	3,000 *nonpassive* income

Your net passive income (loss) is $5,000 (6,000 − 1,000 loss). Correspondingly, your net nonpassive income (loss) is *zero* (3,000 − 2,000 loss − 1,000 loss). The net/net passive/nonpassive income (loss) is $5,000 (5,000 passive + zero nonpassive). The $5,000 was the amount reported to you on the K-1 as Source 1: *Ordinary income (loss) from trade or business activities.* You do this same kind of allocation exercise for other income (loss) sources reported to you Schedule K-1.

Synopsis of Tests 2 Through 7

If an LLC person does not qualify under the 500^+ hours test, he must meet any one of the other six tests to be considered a material participant. Without elaboration, Tests 2 through 7 are enumerated and described in the instructions to Schedule K-1. With Figure 10.2 as our enumeration guide, we'll try to elaborate on the tests in a more meaningful way than the instructions provide.

Test 2 constitutes *substantially all* of the participation required by the activity, regardless of total hours or who else may be involved. If an activity requires only 400 hours of participation for the year, and you provide 350 of those hours, you have materially participated in that activity.

Test 3 is *more than 100 hours* of participation, if no one else contributed a greater amount of time than you. For example, the activity requires 800 hours of participation by all members. You contribute 250 hours and three other members contribute 150 hours each (3 x 150 hours = 450; 450 + 250 = 800). In this case, you would have materially participated.

Test 4 introduces the concept of a *significant participation activity*. Such an activity requires more than 100 hours of some person's time, during the year. If there were three such activities, for example, and your participative time in all three exceeded 500 hours, you qualify as a material participant in all three. Example: 125^+ hours in "A", 150^+ hours in "B", and 225^+ hours in "C", when combined total 500^+ hours. This test is available only if you cannot qualify under any other test.

Test 5 shifts from the yardstick of hours to years. If, in a 10-year period preceding the tax year, you materially participated in the activity for any five years (whether or not consecutive), you qualify. It is not clear whether the five years of participation has to be in the current activity of the partnership, or in a similar activity prior to the partnership. Although this test gives credit for one's "experience" in an activity, we believe it to be the most contentious one for current activity qualification.

Test 6 dwells on *professional service activities*. A professional service activity—

> *involves the performance of personal services in the fields of health, law, engineering, architecture, accounting, actuarial science, performing arts, or any other trade or business in which capital is not a material income-producing factor.*

To qualify under this test, you must have materially participated in the activity for any three years (whether or not consecutive) preceding the tax year.

Test 7 is a catchall where no one test above seems to fit. It's the *facts and circumstances* test: an old standby for the IRS. The official wording leaves much to conscientious judgment; it says—

> *Based on all the facts and circumstances, you participated in the activity on a regular, continuous, and substantial basis during the tax year.*

Disregarded for facts-and-circumstances purposes is "make work" (which has no significant effect on income or loss) and "portfolio time" (with investments not directly related to the day-to-day operations of the activity).

Source 2: Rental Real Estate

The seven material participation tests above were presented within the framework of a trade or business activity: Source 1 income (loss). Now, we want to address Source 2: *Net income (loss) from rental real estate activities*. This is the caption to line 2 in the K-1 instructions. These instructions raise two more participation tests, namely: real estate professional and active participation. We'll address each of these requirements separately. First, the real estate professional.

The instructions to line 2 read, in part—

Generally, the income (loss) reported on line 2 is a passive activity amount for all partners. However, the income (loss) on line 2 is not from a passive activity if you were a real estate professional and you materially participated in the activity. [Emphasis added.]

The point being made by this instruction is that rental real estate (whether residential, commercial, or industrial) is, by definition, a passive activity. (We'll cite the statutory wording on this in our upcoming Chapter 11.) An exception to this general rule applies for real estate professionals. If certain participative conditions are met, said persons are treated as being engaged in a *nonpassive* activity.

A person is a "real estate professional" only if *both* of the following conditions are met:

a. *More than half of the personal services you performed . . . were in real property trades or businesses in which you materially participated and*

b. *You performed more than 750 hours of services in real property trades or businesses.*

The instructions go on to define a real property trade or business as—

any real property development, redevelopment, construction, reconstruction, acquisition, conversion, rental, operation, management, leasing, or brokerage trade or business.

If you are married and filing a joint return with your spouse, each spouse must separately meet both conditions above. That is, each spouse must meet the 750$^+$ hours test on his or her own. If one spouse has 500$^+$ hours and the other has 250$^+$ in real estate activities, the two amounts do not combine to meet the 750$^+$ hours test. Real estate happens to be one of the more common activities where a husband and wife are both engaged therein.

There is a distinct advantage in having a statutorily defined passive activity treated as nonpassive. The passive activity loss rules of Section 469: Passive Activity and Credits Limited, do not apply. As a nonpassive activity, the deductibility of operating losses is limited only by the total positive income generated from other sources (whether K-1 activities or not). We try to make this distinction more graphic in Figure 10.3. Always keep in mind that if you do not make the distinction clear on your part, the IRS will default you to the passive category.

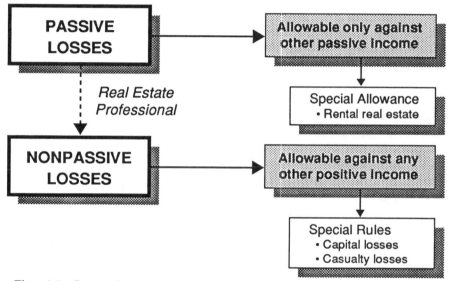

Fig. 10.3 - Synopsis of Distinction Between Passive & Nonpassive Losses

Real Estate "Active Participation"

We are still on the subject of rental real estate: Source 2: line 2 of Schedule K-1. Ordinarily, as a passive activity, losses are allowed only to the extent of passive income. But if certain ownership and other conditions are met, an additional loss up to $25,000 may be allowed. What is the ownership condition?

To qualify for the special $25,000 loss allowance, your ownership interest in the rental realty must not be less than 10% at all times during the tax year. Thus, as an LLC person, if there were

10 equal-owner members of the partnership, each would be a 10% owner of the realty holdings, whatever the rental activities may be. The same 10%-or-more ownership requirement holds true in a proprietorship LLC co-owning rental real estate with non-LLC persons.

The next requirement is *active participation*, by a 10%-or-more owner, in the actual rental activities. Active participation is a less stringent requirement than material participation. It focuses on managerial participation as being quite distinct from personal service participation. Active participation includes approving new tenants, deciding rental terms, approving capital expenditures, overseeing repairs and maintenance, arranging for other services, etc.

Once you satisfy these two requirements, the instructions for line 2 read (as slightly edited)—

If you have a loss from a passive activity on line 2 [of your K-1] and you meet [the active participation requirements], enter the loss on Schedule E (Form 1040), Part II, column (g).

The full caption to column (g) is—

(g) Passive loss allowed
(Attach Form 8582 if required)

Form 8582 is titled: *Passive Activity Loss Limitation*. This form combines the incomes, losses, and loss carryovers of rental real estate activities with those of other passive activities, to establish the net allowable loss for the year at issue. We'll discuss this form in the next chapter.

11

PASSIVE ACTIVITY LOSSES

> **A Passive Activity Is ANY Trade Or Business In Which You Do Not Materially Participate. This Includes Rental Real Estate Activities. The Significance Here Is That The Generation Of Passive Activity Losses Is TAX LIMITED By The Amount Of Passive Activity Income Directly Derived. An Additional Special Loss Allowance (Up To $25,000) May Apply To Rental Real Estate With Active Participation By A 10% Or More LLC Owner. All Unallowed Losses For A Given Year Are Carried Forward To The Following Year. Called "Suspended Losses," They Become A TREASURE TROVE Of Tax Benefits When The Loss Activity Is Ultimately Sold.**

A passive activity, whether in partnership LLC or proprietorship LLC form, carries with it an adverse tax implication. The adverse premise is that in such an activity the owners are motivated primarily by tax benefits at the expense of ordinary profit seeking. This is the rationale behind categorizing trade or business and real estate activities into nonpassive and passive domains. (We discussed the distinction in the preceding chapter.) The presumption is that passive activities are gerrymandered to produce artificially large losses in order to shelter large amounts of nonpassive (positive) income. To overcome this presumption, there is IRC Section 469 to be addressed.

Section 469 is titled: *Passive Activity Losses and Credits Limited.* Its genesis is a flat-out disallowance of losses and credits . . . until certain conditions are met. The statutory essence is that—

Neither (A) the passive activity loss, nor (B) the passive activity credit, shall be allowed . . . for the taxable year [subsec. (a)].

Any loss or credit . . . disallowed under subsection (a) shall be treated as a deduction or credit allocable to such activity in the next taxable year [subsec. (b)].

The computational transition from subsection (a) to subsection (b) spans over 5,000 statutory words. We won't dare mention the word count of the regulations supporting Section 469. We don't need to, because most of the consequences of Section 469 are summarized in **Form 8582**: *Passive Activity Loss Limitations.*

Accordingly, in this chapter we want to focus on the essence of Section 469 as it affects LLC persons only. We particularly want to focus on the arrangement, preparation, and retention (in your records) of Form 8582. There is a secret virtue in this form. If you prepare Form 8582 diligently year after year, at some point in time all cumulative unallowed losses can be used as your "final offset" in a fully taxable transaction. We'll certainly define and explain what would be such a transaction. There is an end-game treasure-trove in what are officially called: *suspended losses.*

Meaning of "Passive Activity"

Keep in mind that Section 469 and Form 8582 apply *only* to passive activities. If you truly materially participated in an LLC activity (as per our Chapter 10), the loss and credit limitation rules do not apply. But, you have to establish clearly your own material participation. Otherwise, as an LLC person, you are automatically construed to be engaged in a passive activity.

Subsection 469(c)(1) makes the above point clear. It states—

The term "passive activity" means any activity—

*(A) which involves the conduct of **any trade or business**, and*
*(B) **in which** the taxpayer **does not** materially participate.* [Emphasis added.]

Although we emphasized the phrase "any trade of business," there is some softening of the disallowance mandate. The disallowance does not apply to non-closely-held C corporations, nor to working interests in oil and gas property. Regular C corporations, particularly those with public stock offerings, are generally not motivated in conducting business operations at a loss. Oil and gas property, by nature, is a speculative business. It rarely attracts nonrecourse capital or those who are preoccupied with limited liability. All other forms of research and experimentation, however, are included as "any activity" constituting a passive activity. The basic distinction between "passive" and "nonpassive" is the absence of direct effort to sell a specific product or service to the general public . . . for profit.

Also included as a passive activity are rental activities such as equipment leasing, real estate structures, farmland rentals, and so on. The term "rental activity" implies that income is generated principally from the *use of property*, rather than from personal services being rendered. The only outright exception to this passivity inclusion is the real estate professional who devotes more than 750 hours per year to real property trades or businesses. In other words, a real estate professional (if tax qualified) is treated as having materially participated in a trade or business. Thus, by "definition in reverse" material participation constitutes a nonpassive activity. This is a restatement of comments made in Chapter 10.

This reverse definition is emphasized in subsection 469(h)(1):

*A taxpayer shall be treated as materially participating in an activity **only if** the taxpayer is involved in the operations of the activity on a basis which is—*

(A) regular,
(B) continuous, and
(C) substantial.

If one is not engaged in an activity on a regular, continuous, and substantial basis, he is — by default — engaged in a passive activity. Having an ownership interest in a purely passive activity is tax disadvantageous. You'll see why subsequently below.

Commentary on Rental Activities

Unless shown otherwise, a rental activity is construed to be a passive activity. This is so, regardless of an owner's participation in the activity. A "rental activity" exists where (1) tangible property is used by, or held for use by, customers and (2) the gross income therefrom represents amounts paid, or to be paid, for the use of such property. This is the regulatory substance of Section 469(c)(2): *Passive activity includes any rental activity.*

Regulation § 1.469-1T(e)(3) sets out certain exceptions where property is used by *customers*, in contrast to its use by tenants. Catering to customers is more analogous to a nonpassive trade or business; they come and go on a short-term basis: almost always less than 30 days. A "tenant" wants to retain use of the property for much longer periods of time: typically, one year or more. For customers, the rental agreement is oral and by annotations in a daily log. For tenants, the rental agreement is in the form of a written legal contract.

The first exception to the passive activity rule on rentals is customer use for seven days or less. This exception serves to exclude most auto, tuxedo, and videocassette rentals. It also excludes short-term use of hotel, motel, and bed and breakfast facilities. The rationale for this exception is that the person furnishing the property for such short-term rental is required to provide sufficient services to justify the conclusion that it is a service business rather than a rental activity.

The second exception (to the passive activity rule) applies when the average period of customer use is 30 days or less. Here, the rationale is that significant, if not extraordinary, services are required to maintain the property and accommodate the special needs of each customer. For example, vacation rentals in resort areas, hospital rooms and convalescent homes, and temporary housing pending the sale of property.

A third exception pertains to rentals that are incidental to nonrental activities. The best example is lodging furnished to employees for convenience of the employer. Examples are rooms on shipboard in international trade, rooms on oil rigs in offshore sites, rooms in gambling casinos for 24-hour on-call employees, and other similar employer needs. As a rule of thumb, the term "incidental" means that the fair rental value of such property is 2 percent or less of the gross income of the nonrental activities.

There are a few other exceptions such as the use of a golf course, conducting seminars, show rooms, displaying property for sale, and so on. The common thread to all exceptions is that while property is being "rented" in the technical sense, the services provided are regular, continuous, and substantial. This is the foundation of any ordinary trade or business.

Passive Activity Gross Income

There is a planning strategy that pervades all those who hold ownership interests in one or more passive activities. Once aware that passive activity losses are limited by the amount of passive activity income generated for the year, there is a desire to assign various extraneous sources of income to the passive activity category. While many of those sources may indeed be passive, they do not constitute passive activity income as defined by IRC Section 469(e) and its supporting regulations. The cardinal rule on point is Regulation § 1.469-2T(c)(1). It reads—

*Except as otherwise provided in the regulations under section 469, passive activity gross income for a taxable year includes any item of gross income **if and only if** such income **is from a** passive activity.* [Emphasis added.]

The most common source of passive income which is **not** classed as passive activity income pertains to "portfolio income." This is income which one derives from nontrade and nonbusiness investments. One makes purely passive investments to produce income: not to generate losses. Such income is in the form of interest, dividends, royalties, annuities, capital gains, and return of capital. Although there is some risk involved, the money used for ordinary personal investment, and the attention required to protect it, is not the type of activity that is analogous to an LLC trade or business or that is required for the purchase of property for rental to tenants and customers.

In some LLC arrangements, it is difficult to distinguish between portfolio income, nonpassive activity income, and passive activity income. Attribution difficulties arise when one loans money to an entity in which he has an ownership interest, when property not used in a trade or business is sold or exchanged, when personal services are rendered, when accounting changes are made, when refunds, rebates, and insurance proceeds are received, when there is income from covenants not to compete, or when there is income from estates and trusts. There are regulations which address each of these types of income. But they are too numerous and too complicated for presentation here. Instead, we try to present in Figure 11.1 the basic distinguishing features for each class of income: portfolio, nonpassive, passive, and other.

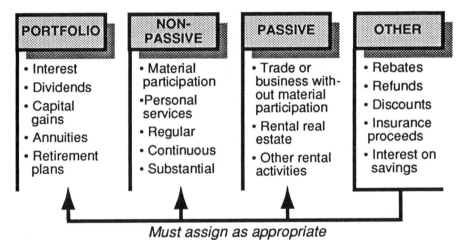

Must assign as appropriate

Fig. 11.1 - Comparative Types of Income from LLC Activities

In general, the personal and business relationships between LLC members are close and interchangeable. There is a strong temptation to assign the components of entity income to those classes which do them the most tax good. If not done with intentional deception, there is nothing wrong with so doing. However, be aware that under subsection 469(l): *Regulations*, the IRS has authority to recharacterize income to more appropriately reflect the provisions of Section 469. This means that some of the income you may have designated as "passive" could be recharacterized as portfolio income or as nonpassive activity income. Portfolio income has its own rules for the netting and taxing of income, gains, and losses. Separate income and loss rules apply also to nonpassive activity income. Any net, nonpassive income from an LLC arrangement carries its burden of social security and medicare taxes, in addition to its ordinary income taxes.

Passive Activity Deductions

As with passive activity income, passive activity deductions must relate directly to the passive activity for which ordinary and necessary expenses are incurred. As such, the deductions become allowable as an offset against passive activity income. The result is net income or net loss for the taxable year. If there is more than one passive activity in the LLC arrangement, the net income or net loss for each activity must be established separately. When selling a separate passive activity, all applicable losses can be deducted. All nets are then aggregated for pass-through reporting purposes.

More formally, a deduction is a passive activity deduction if it either (1) arises in connection with the conduct of a passive activity for the tax year, or (2) is a passive activity loss carried forward from a prior tax year. Examples of allowable deductions are advertising expenses, car and truck expenses, commissions paid, depreciation allowances, liability insurance, legal and professional fees, materials and supplies, maintenance and repairs, property taxes and business licenses, mortgage and other interest, utilities, wages paid, travel and entertainment, and other necessary operating expenditures.

Items specifically *excluded* from passive activity deductions are:

(1)   those clearly and directly allocable to portfolio income;
(2)   losses from the disposition of portfolio income property;
(3)   losses from dispositions of passive activity interests to related parties;
(4)   mortgage interest on property used for the personal benefit of LLC owners;
(5)   state, local, or foreign income taxes;
(6)   net operating loss carrybacks or carryovers;
(7)   casualty and theft losses;

(8) expenses in anticipation of commencing a passive activity; and

(9) interest paid on debt proceeds used for *other than* specific expenditures for a passive activity.

Special $25,000 Loss Allowance

The above narration on income and deductions for a passive activity applies to the LLC entity which owns and operates the passive activity (or activities). After any aggregate net *loss* is passed through prorata to the LLC members, another form of loss allowance may apply. This is the *$25,000 Offset for Rental Real Estate Activities* prescribed by IRC Section 469(i). The word count on this subsection is over 1,250 words. Thus, we resort here to presenting its essence only.

The $25,000 loss offset is allowable only to individuals and their estates (up to two years after death). If an individual is married, but filing a separate return from his spouse (and living separately all year), the allowable offset amount is $12,500. Married persons filing separate returns, who lived with their spouses at any time during the year, are not eligible for any part of the special allowance. Otherwise, the full offset amount is allowed where an individual's AGI (Adjusted Gross Income) on Form 1040 is $100,000 or less. The allowable amount "phases out" between $100,000 and $150,000 of AGI, and disappears altogether for AGIs over $150,000.

Aside from the AGI aspects, eligibility for the $25,000 loss offset requires that an LLC member "actively participate" in the management affairs of the rental real estate activity or activities. Such participation consists of (a) approving new tenants, (b) deciding on rental terms, (c) approving capital or repair expenditures, and (d) resolving tenant complaints. No specific minimum hours are required, so long as the participation is consistent and continuous throughout each rental year.

Additionally, an eligible LLC member must have at least 10% or more ownership interest in each rental activity which sustains a net loss for the year. Thus, if there were two or more eligible LLC members, each, separately, could qualify for all or part of the

$25,000 special loss allowance. This, alone, is a persuasive reason for an LLC arrangement to include one or more rental real estate activities.

Form 8582: Purpose & Overview

In order to establish the deductible amount of the $25,000 special loss allowance, Form 8582 is required. This form is titled: *Passive Activity Loss Limitations*. This form can only be used by noncorporate taxpayers: individuals, estates, and trusts. Its purpose is twofold. One purpose is to compute the total (aggregate) passive activity losses that are allowable for the current year. Its second purpose is to provide an accounting methodology for tracking those unallowable losses (called: *suspended* losses) which are carryoverable to the subsequent year or years. The current year total losses allowed are shown on page 1 of the form. The suspended losses are detailed on various worksheets which parallel the entries on page 1. Only page 1 of Form 8582 — not the worksheets — is attached to Form 1040 when it is filed.

An abbreviated arrangement of Form 8582 is presented in Figure 11.2. Note that it consists of three parts: I, II, and III. Part I consists of two subparts, which separate rental real estate activities from all other passive activities. Both subparts have the same format, namely:

a. *Activities with net income* _____

b. *Activities with net loss* < _____ >

c. *Prior years unallowed losses* < _____ >

d. *Combine the above* _____

The two subpart combinations are then combined to comprise line 3 on Form 8582. Our Figure 11.2 displays all of the official line numbers. We refer to these lines below.

If line 3 **and** line 1d (rental real estate activities with active participation) both are losses, Part II comes into play. Part II focuses on the $25,000 special loss allowance for rental real estate activities. Part II computes an additional allowable loss beyond that allowable in Part I.

Form 8582	PASSIVE ACTIVITY LOSS LIMITATIONS		Year
	See preprinted instructions on face of official form		

Part I	Aggregate Passive Activity Loss		
Rental Real Estate Activities With Active Participation	1a. With net income		
	1b. With net loss	< >	
	1c. Prior unallowed losses	< >	
	1d. Combine lines 1a, 1b, & 1c ➞ 1d.		
All Other Passive Activities	2a. With net income		
	2b. With net loss	< >	
	2c. Prior unallowed losses	< >	
	2d. Combine lines 2a, 2b, & 2c ➞ 2d.		
	3. Combine lines 1d and 2d ➞ 3.		

Part II	Special Allowance Re Rental Real Estate	
4.	SMALLER of <u>loss</u> on line 1d or <u>loss</u> on line 3 ➞ 4.	
5.	If married filing jointly ----------------------	$150,000
6.	Enter **Modified AGI** --------------------	
7.	Subtract line 6 from line 5	
8.	Multiply line 7 by 50% - Enter no more than $25,000	
9.	SMALLER of line 4 or line 8 ---------------- ➞ 9.	

Part III	Total Losses Allowed : Current Year	
10.	Add <u>income</u>, if any, on lines 1a & 2a ---------- ➞ 10.	
11.	Add lines 9 & 10	**TOTAL LOSSES ALLOWED ▶**

Part I losses minus Part III allowed, equal carryover losses

Fig. 11.2 - Abbreviated Arrangement of Form 8582

The Part I allowable loss equals the sum of the income amounts (if any) entered on line 1a (real estate activities) and on line 2a (all other passive activities). To this amount, there is added the amount (if any) appearing on line 9 of Part II. Part III adds the Part I and Part II losses together to become *Total losses allowed* for the current year. If the total losses in Part I exceed those allowed in Part III, the excess is unallowed and is carried forward.

Also Form 8582-CR

The passive activity rules impose limitations not only on the amount of losses and deductions allowable, but also on the amount of credits allowable. In the context used here, a "credit" is an allowable offset (dollar-for-dollar) against the regular tax on income. Generally, a tax credit is a statutory incentive for undertaking certain forms of business investment in disadvantaged sectors of the national economy and of society. Where passive activities are involved, the IRS document for claiming, computing, and tracking the allowability of applicable credits is Form 8582-CR (the "CR" is for "credit" . . . obviously). Said form is titled: *Passive Activity Credit Limitations*.

Form 8582-CR is considerably more complicated than Form 8582 for loss limitations. The primary reason for this is that there are so many potentially allowable credits. There are at least nine. Each authorized credit has its own tax law, own regulations, and own tax form. The computing and tracking of each credit becomes a separate worksheet for supporting the entries on Form 8582-CR. Indeed, the approximately 14,000 words of instructions to Form 8582-CR prescribe *nine separate worksheets* if all potential credits are sought. Each credit worksheet is columned into: (1) name of activity; (2) from credit form number (from list below); (3) current year tentative credits; (4) prior year unallowed credits; (5) total credits available; (6) current year credits allowable; and (7) credit carryovers to subsequent year.

What is the nature of the credits potentially allowable? There are such credits as—

- Work opportunity credit (Form 5884),
- Low-income housing credit (Form 8586),
- Disabled access credit (Form 8826),
- Empowerment zone employment credit (Form 8844),
- Community development credit (Form 8847),
- Credit for alcohol fuel used (Form 6478),
- Renewable electricity production credit (Form 8835),
- Credit for increasing research activities (Form 6765),
. . . and others

These types of credits are coveted mostly by registered tax shelter activities in the form of *Publicly Traded Partnerships* (PTPs). PTP investors are especially attracted to "multiply bundled" tax credits promoted and managed with corporate accounting expertise. Without much effort on the investors' part, legitimate tax offsets can accrue.

In contrast, LLC persons are more managerially active on their own. They tend to be easily frustrated with each credit's tax law and its qualifying rules. Consider, for example, the low-income housing credit: IRC Section 42. For non-federally-subsidized new residential rental property, there's a credit of 70% of its "qualified basis" over a 10-year period. A credit of this magnitude is extremely attractive; would you not agree? BUT, to claim it properly one has to review the 20,000 words of statutory text and the 125 pages of IRS regulations, rulings, and procedures. If you are up to it, that's great. Get Form 8586: *Low-Income Housing Credit*, then proceed. In the meantime, we are going to bypass Form 8582-CR in its entirety.

Back to Part I, Form 8582

Form 8582 is accompanied by over 12,000 words of instructions. Titled: *Instructions for Form 8582*, most are quite informative. We certainly urge that you — as an LLC person — procure and read them. In said instructions you are reminded that Form 8582 is required only—

When total losses (including prior year unallowed losses) from all your passive activities exceed the total income from all your passive activities.

There is no way of knowing this, until after you have completed Part I of Form 8582. Part I summarizes the income and losses from all passive activities: rental real estate and other.

On the official form, the words on lines 1a, 1b, 2a, and 2b (in Figure 11.2) commence with: *Activities*. . . .This is a plural term. It implies that you may have more than one activity for line 1 (rental real estate with active participation) and/or more than one activity for line 2 (all other passive activities). Indeed, you might. And, indeed you should with an LLC arrangement.

Under the subheading: *Grouping of Activities*, in the instructions, you may combine certain activities when they constitute a *single economic unit*. Such a unit is one which can be sold, exchanged, or dissolved on its own without affecting the account records of other activities in the LLC operation. Accordingly, each economic unit should be a separate "cost center" with its own worksheets and backup records. Not only does this foster disciplined bookkeeping, it enables selected LLC members to become active participants in designated activities and become passive participants in other activities.

With the above in mind, we revisit Part I of Form 8582 and present it as Figure 11.3. Note that we show five separate passive activities: A, B, C, D, and E. We do this to illustrate the flexibility of an LLC. Furthermore, note that we indicate that separate worksheets are kept on each activity showing its net income or net loss for the current year, plus each activity's prior year unallowed losses. With such worksheets, it is a simple matter to "plug in" the income and losses on lines 1 and 2. You can prepare your own worksheets or follow the official instructions for doing so.

Line 3 is where most thought is required. If line 3 shows a net income or zero, Form 8582 becomes another addition to your worksheet records. All losses are allowed, including any prior unallowed losses.

Only if line 3 **and** 1d both are losses do you go to Part II. This part, recall, is titled: *Special* [Loss] *Allowance for Rental Real Estate Activities with Active Participation*. If line 1d shows net income, when line 3 shows a net loss, Part II does not apply.

More on Part II

Part II of Form 8582 requires additional information beyond that in Figure 11.2. The entry and computational aspects are self-explanatory (especially on the official form), but some background commentary is needed.

First off, all entries in Part II are positive numbers even though loss amounts appear at lines 4, 8, and 9 (recall Figure 11.2). This is

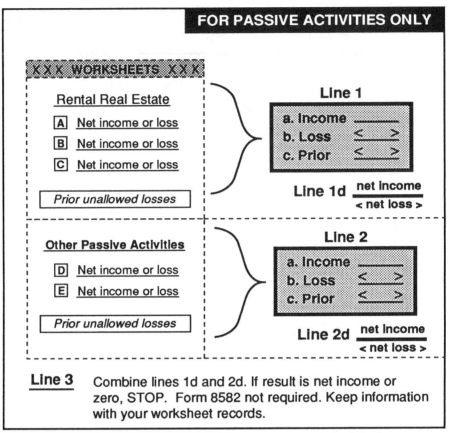

Fig. 11.3 - Part I of Form 8582 Separated and Revisited

simply to avoid algebraic confusion in Part II. Furthermore, a special headnote says—

> *If your filing status is married filing separately and you **lived with** your spouse at any time during the year, **do not** complete Part II. Instead, enter -0- [zero] on line 9 and go to line 10.*

Caution is required on line 5. Instead of entering $150,000 for married filing jointly, if you are married filing separately and you **lived apart** from your spouse at all times during the year, enter $75,000. Line 5 is the reference base for the phaseout of the special loss allowance for AGIs over $100,000 married filing jointly, or over $75,000 for married filing separately (when living apart).

Line 6: *Modified* AGI (adjusted gross income) requires that you read the official instructions. In most cases, though, your modified AGI is your regular AGI (at the bottom of Form 1040) *before* entry of any Form 8582 losses, and after subtracting any taxable social security income. If your regular AGI includes any IRA deduction, student loan interest deduction, one-half self-employment tax deduction, exclusion for series EE bonds, or exclusion for child adoptions, these items are **added back** to establish your modified AGI. Obviously, if your modified AGI is equal to or greater than $150,000 [line 5], you get no special loss allowance. You skip lines 7 and 8, enter -0- [zero] on line 9, and go to line 10 (in Part III).

What is not made clear in Part II is that, if your modified AGI is less than $100,000 married filing jointly, or less than $50,000 married filing separately living apart all year, Part II may not apply. In fact, if your only passive losses are from rental real estate activities with active participation, and they total not more than $25,000 ($12,500 for married filing separately, living apart), no Form 8582 is required at all. This is described as *Exception 2* in the instructions to Form 8582.

More on Part III

Part III of Form 8582 consists of lines 10 and 11 (recall Figure 11.2 again). The preprinted instructions on the official form are self-explanatory, as far as they go. The amount shown on line 11 is the: *Total losses allowed from all passive activities*, for the current tax year. It is one aggregate amount only. If you have five separate passive activities as we depict in Figure 11.3, how do you allocate the total loss allowed to the five activities?

Answer: This is where your worksheets to Part I and accounting common sense come in handy. Let us illustrate with simple numbers.

Suppose that Part III shows the total losses allowed to be <$9,000>. And, further, suppose that your worksheets to Part I indicate as follows:

Activity	Income	Loss	Prior Unallowed	Net Income/Loss
A		<3,500>	<2.500>	<6,000>
B	5,000		<1,000>	4,000
C		<6,500>	<1,500>	<8,000>
D	12,000			12,000
E		<9,000>	<8,000>	<17,000>
			Net total actual losses	<15,000>

Hence, we have $15,000 of net actual current year losses among five activities, of which only $9,000 is allowable. How do we allocate the $9,000 allowable and account for the unallowed losses?

We allocate the $9,000 of allowable loss to the net *loss* activities only: A, C, and E above. The net income activities, B and D, "take care of themselves" on the tax forms and schedules. We allocate to A, C, and E, proportionately, as follows:

Activity	Net Loss	Allowable Ratio	Allowable Amount	Unallowed Amount
A	<6,000>	0.1935	<1,740>	<4,260>
C	<8,000>	0.2580	<2,322>	<5,676>
E	<17,000>	0.5485	<4,938>	<12,064>
Totals	<31,000>	1.0000	<9,000>	<22,000>

The total loss of the loss activities A, C, and E for the current year [<31,000>] includes the allocable prior year unallowed losses for each loss activity [the <2,500>, <1,500>, <8,000> = <12,000> in the "prior unallowed" column above]. Without these prior year unallowed losses, the current year losses for A, C, and E total <19,000> [the <3,500> + <6,500> + <9,000> in the "loss column" above].

Since only $9,000 of $19,000 current year loss is allowable, that leaves $10,000 of current year losses unallowed. This $10,000 of unallowed losses attaches to the $12,000 of prior year unallowed losses to become $22,000 of *cumulative* unallowed losses. We show the allocation effect of these "suspended" losses in the "Unallowed Amount" column above. The allocated suspended losses are carried over to the worksheets of the subsequent year Form 8582. The allocated loss carryovers continue year after year, until each passive activity is disposed of in a fully taxable transaction.

"Triggering" of Suspended Losses

When a passive activity is sold in a fully taxable transaction, the event is characterized as a disposition. That is, all ownership interests in that activity are transferred to a new owner (or owners). If the new owner is unrelated (by family or business arrangements) to the transferor, all suspended passive activity losses are "triggered" at that time. This means that such losses can be used to offset income or gain from nonpassive activities.

How so? It's there in Section 469(g): *Dispositions of Entire Interest in Passive Activity*. The substance of this 300-word subsection is that—

*If all gain or loss realized on such disposition is recognized, **the excess of any loss from such activity (determined after the** [prior year unallowed loss carryovers are applied]), over the net income or gain from all other passive activities . . . shall be treated as a loss which is not from a passive activity*. [Emphasis added.]

In other words, in a bona fide sale, all passive loss accounting up to the day before date of sale is treated under the Form 8582 rules. On date of sale, transfer of ownership occurs. At that time, different accounting rules come into play. The suspended losses are wiped clean!

To illustrate how the triggering concept works, take a look at your latest Form 1040: *U.S. Individual Income Tax Return*. On its page 1, you'll find such items there as—

* *Wages and salaries,*
* *Interest and dividends,*

- *Business income or (loss)*
- *Capital gain or (loss)*
- ***Other gains or (losses): Form 4797***
- *Rents, royalties, partnerships . . . etc.*

When the sale of a passive loss business is consummated, the disposition event is reported on Form 4797: ***Sales of Business Property***. This is a truly unique form. If a net loss results from the sale of a passive activity, it "self-converts" from a capital loss to an ordinary loss [Subsec. 1231(a)(2)]. As an ordinary loss, there is no limitation on its use as an offset against nonpassive sources of income or gain that are entered in Form 1040. This is why there is a separate line (as shown above) on Form 1040 to accommodate the results of Form 4797.

The carrying forward of suspended losses year after year can become a disconcerting chore. The bookkeeping tends to get sloppy . . . or not done at all. The loss activity becomes an albatross to the overall LLC operation. At some point, some impatient member says: "Let's get rid of the darn thing!"

Which brings us to our final point in this chapter. Suspended losses become an end-game treasure-trove. If there are any usable assets of the activity at all, they can be sold at some price — albeit in distress. Even selling in good faith for $1 to an unrelated third party constitutes a bona fide sale.

Using activity E above with its suspended loss (unallowed amount) of <$12,064>, here's how the end-game works out. The following pertinent entries on Form 4797 are made:

Col. (d) —	*Gross sales price*	$ *1*
Col. (e) —	*Depreciation allowed/allowable*	*-0-*
Col. (f) —	*Cost or other basis*	*12,064*
Col. (g) —	*Gain or loss*	*<12,063>*

Suspended losses ADD TO BASIS at time of a fully taxable disposition. Once you realize this, preprinted instructions on Form 4797 direct you how to convert the loss to an ordinary loss, and report it as such on Form 1040.

12

FOREIGN ENTITY LLCs

A Foreign LLC Is An Unincorporated Entity Created And Organized Under Foreign Law. Through A U.S. Manager, It Can Elect Its Form Of Tax Treatment When Conducting A Trade Or Business In The U.S. The Most Common Such Treatment Is That Of A Partnership Where The "Pass-Through" Principles Of Distributive Sharing With Foreign Members Apply. At The End Of A Foreign LLC's Tax Accounting Year, Stringent WITHHOLDING AT SOURCE Rules Apply. The Idea Is To Over-Withhold Tax So As To "Dollar Carrot" Each Foreign LLC Member To File For A Refund, By Using Form 1040NR: U.S. Nonresident Alien Income Tax Return.

For LLC purposes, an "eligible entity" — whether domestic or foreign — is a for-profit business which is not a corporation. A domestic entity is one created or organized in the U.S., or under a law of the U.S., or under a law of any state of the U.S. An entity is foreign if it is not domestic. Not all foreign entities, however, are eligible for LLC treatment. IRS Regulation § 301.7701-2(b)(8) lists some 80+ foreign entities as *per se corporations*. The "per se" means having more characteristics of a U.S. corporation than those of an unincorporated U.S. enterprise. Except for the IRS listed per se entities, all other business arrangements of foreign origin are eligible for LLC treatment under U.S. tax laws.

Foreign entities conducting LLC business within the U.S. are subject to U.S. tax laws under two commonly recognized international taxation principles. One principle addresses that income which is *effectively connected with* a trade or business in the U.S. The entity and owners are subject to the same tax rates and benefits as are U.S. citizens and domestic LLCs. The second principle addresses that income which is *fixed or determinable from* sources within the U.S. (from other than a trade or business). The fixed or determinable income is taxed at a flat 30% rate, or at a lower rate if there is a Tax Treaty in effect. The U.S. has entered into agreements with some 65+ sovereign nations with the objective of minimizing any double taxation to those foreign citizens and entities. Such is an "objective" only.

Accordingly, in this our final chapter, we want to explore with you the tax ramifications (rules and forms, etc.) of eligible foreign entities electing LLC status in the U.S. As the world becomes more reciprocal-trade oriented, we should expect more unincorporated foreign interests seeking entrepreneurial opportunities in the U.S. The U.S. is probably the most lucrative open market in the world. Consequently, we want to focus strictly on foreign LLC activities in the U.S. Such entities and their owners face the daunting task of filing U.S. income tax returns and paying U.S. taxes, then, separately, having to deal with their own national tax authorities for avoiding or minimizing any double taxation. Although our emphasis is clearly on the federal treatment of foreign LLCs, we'll express a comment or two about state law treatment thereof.

Same Elective Options Apply

Whether a business arrangement is an entity separate from its owners for federal tax purposes is a matter of federal tax law. This jurisdiction is independent of whether the arrangement is recognized under state law or under foreign law. Therefore, the pertinent applicable federal rule is IRS Regulation § 301.7701-3(b)(2): *Classification of eligible entities that do not file an election; Foreign eligible entities.* Paragraph (i) of this rule reads:

Unless the entity elects otherwise, a foreign eligible entity is—

(A) A partnership if it has two or more members and at least one member does not have limited liability;

(B) An association if all members have limited liability; or

(C) Disregarded as an entity separate from its owner if it has a single owner that does not have limited liability.

Paragraph (ii) of said rule defines limited liability. It reads:

A member of a foreign eligible entity has limited liability if the member has no personal liability for the debts of or claims against the entity by reason of being a member. This determination is based solely on the statute or law pursuant to which the entity is organized.

When organized under foreign law, it is seldom clear as to the extent of personal liability imposed, or whether such liability is limited or not. In most cases, foreign organizational laws are silent on these matters. One reason for this silence is that no other nation in the world is as litigation driven as is the U.S. Furthermore, on matters of business law, the legal interpretation of words and phrases in a law are not universally accepted. Language and customs play a major interpretive role.

Fortunately, the foreign law situation is not as unmanageable as it appears. Any foreign entity doing business in any state of the U.S. must *register* with the Secretary of that state. Once registered as an LLC, the foreign entity must comply with that state's LLC law just like any domestic LLC.

Meanwhile, at the federal level, IRS Form 8832: *Entity Classification Election*, is applicable. We discussed this form in detail back in Chapter 4. On said form, three checkboxes are intended solely for foreign entities. The captions to these particular checkboxes read:

☐ *A foreign eligible entity electing to be classed as an association taxable as a* **corporation***.*

☐ *A foreign eligible entity electing to be classified as a* **partnership***.*

☐ *A foreign eligible entity with a single owner electing to be disregarded as a separate entity* [that is, a proprietorship].

Thus, an eligible foreign entity can elect its U.S. tax classification, the same way — on the same form — that a domestic LLC uses. The only obstacle to a foreign entity is knowing the existence of, and gaining access to, Form 8832.

Effective Date & Relevance

Form 8832 is executed upon the affixing of authorized signatures to the Consent Statement to be U.S. taxed as elected. The authorizing signatures are either:

(A) Each member of the electing entity who is an owner at the time the election is filed; OR

(B) Any officer, manager, or member of the electing entity who is authorized (under local law or the entity's organizational documents) to make the election and who represents to having such authorization.

The authorizing agent must also assure the IRS that no *extraordinary transaction* has taken place. Such would occur if 10% or more of foreign ownership interests have been sold, exchanged, or transferred in the U.S.

An eligible entity created or organized under foreign law, whose owner-members are foreign citizens, would unlikely, on its own, know about IRS Form 8832. It is reasonable, therefore, to assume that one or more such members would have made at least some preliminary contact with a U.S. business correspondent. The U.S. person or entity could be authorized to be an on-site manager to get the LLC ball rolling. A U.S. manager does not have to be a member of the foreign LLC. He could be a paid manager with the proper authorizing documents and contract.

At some point, a U.S. manager of a foreign LLC has to establish the "effective date" for commencing business in the U.S. This is line 3 on Form 8832, to wit—

Election is to be effective beginning (month, day, year) (see instructions) ▶ ___/___/___

The instructions point out that the effective date is that which is entered on line 3, or if no entry is made, the date of filing with the IRS Service Center in Philadelphia, PA. The instructions further state that—

An election . . . can take effect no more than 75 days prior to the date the election is filed, nor can it take effect later than 12 months after the date on which the election is filed.

This "grace period" of 75 days before, or 12 months after, filing Form 8832 should provide ample time to work out initial business arrangements, getting a U.S. Tax I.D., and perhaps even setting up a U.S. bank account. During this period, there is the issue of "relevance" to be addressed.

The effective date for U.S. tax compliance purposes is set by events which lead to the first U.S. dollar being obligated to be paid to the foreign entity. This is where Regulation § 301.7701-3(d)1): *Foreign entity relevance*, comes in. The substance of this regulation is that—

A foreign eligible entity's classification is relevant when its classification affects the liability of any person for federal tax or information purposes. [It is that date on which] *an event occurs that creates an obligation to file a federal tax return, information return, or statement for which the classification of the entity must be determined.*

There is an ideal way to document this "relevant date." Have the U.S. paying source write a check payable to the foreign entity in its LLC name. Have the U.S. manager make a photocopy of this check. Then, using the U.S. Tax I.D., set up a U.S. bank account, and deposit that check. Keep the deposit receipt as the date of verification of what took place. This need only be done for the first U.S. income source event. This and other relevant matters are depicted, for instructional summary purposes, in Figure 12.1.

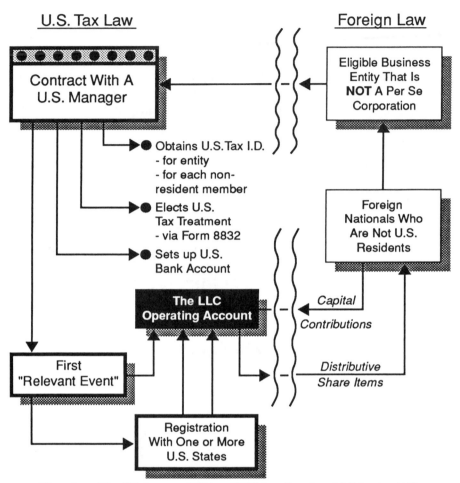

Fig. 12.1 - The "Scheme of Things" With a Foreign LLC in the U.S.

Registering with Each State

All 50 states of the U.S. recognize Form 8832 as evidence of a foreign LLC's federal tax classification. Said form, however, is no substitute for each state's separate law for transacting business within its boundaries. Each state has its own registration procedures. If doing business in more than one U.S. state is intended, registration with each such state is necessary.

Typically, the state-law prerequisites are—

1. Before transacting intrastate business in this state, a foreign limited liability company shall register with the Secretary of State.

2. The laws of the state or foreign country under which a foreign LLC is organized shall govern its organization and internal affairs and the liability and authority of its managers and members.

3. A foreign LLC may not be denied registration by reason of any difference between those laws and the laws of this state.

4. Annexed to the application for registration shall be a certificate from an authorized public official of the foreign LLC's jurisdiction of organization to the effect that the foreign LLC is in good standing in that jurisdiction.

5. In order to register, a foreign LLC shall submit to the Secretary of State application for registering as a foreign LLC, signed by a person with authority to do so under the laws of the state of its organization, on a form prescribed by the Secretary of State.

[Excerpts from California LLC law, Chapter 10: Foreign Limited Liability Companies; Sections 17450 through 17457.]

In the case of California, there is an officially prescribed Form LLC-5: *Limited Liability Company Application for Registration*. Among other items, the form requires designation of the name under which the foreign LLC proposes to register and transact business, the state or country under whose laws it was formed, its date of formation, an agent within the state for service of process, the principal office in-state, and the type of business intended. When the filing fee is paid and all papers are in order, a Certificate of Registration is issued. Thereafter, the foreign LLC may conduct business, file tax forms and information returns, just like any other domestic LLC. Recall Chapters 2 and 3 in this regard.

Federal Form 1065 Revisited

Back in Chapter 5, we addressed various tax forms and schedules applicable to a domestic LLC. As pointed out then, the applicable federal form when there are two or more LLC members is Form 1065: *U.S. Return of Partnership Income.* Elsewhere, we pointed out that until the Internal Revenue Code is amended to expressly accommodate limited liability companies, the "partnership model" is to be used. Even with this model, there is no separate form (such as 1065-F) for a foreign partnership. Consequently, whether an LLC or a partnership, domestic or foreign, Form 1065 is entity required.

The only IRS-recognized evidence on Form 1065 that designates it as an LLC return is its Schedule B (on page 2): *Other Information.* At Question 1, there is a checkbox for signifying a domestic LLC and another for signifying a foreign partnership. There is no checkbox preprinted: Foreign LLC. There is, however, a blank checkbox labeled: *Other* ▶ _____. The clear intention is that one check the box at the blank line, then enter: *Foreign limited liability company.* Rather than using the letters "LLC," we suggest spelling out the whole term.

In addition to the above, there are 11 other questions on Schedule B (1065). They are checkbox answerable "Yes" or No". Some are self-explanatory; some are not applicable. Others require some explanation on our part. When reading any of the questions, you have to mentally translate the word "partner" into "LLC member," and word "partnership" into "LLC partnership" or "LLC entity."

For example, Question 3 as translated reads:

Did the partnership [LLC entity] *own any interest in another partnership* [LLC entity] *or in any foreign entity that was disregarded as an entity separate from its owner under Regulations . . .?* ☐ *Yes* ☐ *No*

While answering this question may be straightforward, the reason for asking it may not be apparent. The IRS concern is the potential for "switching money" between entities (from U.S. based foreign LLCs to foreign based entities and LLCs) in an endeavor to avoid U.S. income tax. There is nothing inherently wrong with transferring money and property overseas so long as the rules for *Withholding of Tax on Nonresident Aliens and Foreign Corporations* are followed [IRC Sections 1441 through 1446].

A more direct inquiry pertaining to money and property transfers overseas is Question 6. It reads quite simply—

> *Does this partnership* [LLC entity] *have any foreign partners* [LLC members]? ☐ *Yes* ☐ *No*

Surely, a foreign LLC would have foreign members: some or all as individuals, or some or all as entities. When answering "Yes" to this question, the IRS computer searches for compliance with the "withholding of tax" rules referenced above. We'll expand on these rules later. In the meantime, we present Figure 12.2 as means for focusing on the importance of Schedule B (Form 1065) for foreign entity LLCs.

Foreign Accounts Question

We are continuing with Schedule B (1065). The last of the questions are 9, 10, 11, and 12. All are directed at foreign financial accounts, foreign trusts, foreign business entities, and foreign correspondents. Most surely, a U.S. based foreign LLC would have one or more types of financial arrangements with its foreign owners and investors. As nonresidents of the U.S., they have their own local bank accounts and regional financial institutions.

Instead of citing the questions in the "partnership language" in which they are printed on Schedule B (1065), we'll paraphrase them as though they were written expressly for LLCs. In this vein, Question 9 reads:

> *Did the LLC have an interest in or a signature or other authority over a financial account in a foreign country?* ☐ *Yes* ☐ *No. If "Yes," enter name of country and see filing requirements for Form TD F 90-22.1* ▶ _____

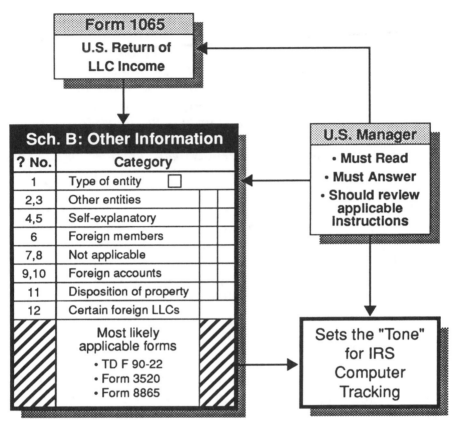

Fig. 12.2 - Categorizing the 12 "Must Answer" Questions on Sch. B (1065)

Form TD F 90-22.1 is **not** an IRS form. It is a Treasury Department form (hence the "TD"; the "F" is "foreign"); when completed, it is mailed directly to the Department of Treasury at the address preprinted on the lower portion of each page of the form. Form TD F 90-22.1 is required only if the aggregate value in all accounts in foreign countries exceeds U.S. $10,000. The form is titled: ***Report of Foreign Bank and Financial Accounts***. It asks for the number of foreign accounts, the type and maximum value of each (by checkboxes), each account number, the name of each account owner, the name of the foreign bank or financial institution, and the country where each account is held.

Question 10 on Schedule B (1065) reads:

Did the LLC receive a distribution from, or was it the grantor of, or transferor to, a foreign trust? ☐ *Yes* ☐ *No. If "Yes," see instructions for the filing of Form 3520.*

Form 3520 is an IRS form and is titled: **Annual Return to Report Transactions with Foreign Trusts and Receipt of Certain Foreign Gifts.** This is a very formidable form. It consists of six pages of tax and financial information and is supplemented by 12 pages of instructional text. If your LLC transfers any money to a foreign **trust** or receives a distribution from one, filing is required. The form is not intended for ordinary business transactions between the LLC entity in the U.S. and its owner-members resident in foreign countries. Transactions with foreign trusts *imply* tax avoidance motivations.

Question 11 reads:

Was there a distribution of property or a transfer (by sale or death) of an LLC interest? ☐ *Yes* ☐ *No. If "Yes," the LLC may elect to adjust the basis of the LLC assets under Section 754* [re adjustment to basis].

When there is a transfer of LLC ownership interests by sale or death, the new acquirer of those interests will have a higher relative percentage of ownership than the continuing members. This arises because, more often, the transfer(s) take place at higher market valuations than the contributing value by the transferor. This puts the continuing members at a disadvantage, relatively, until the basis of the LLC assets are readjusted. IRC Section 754: **Manner of Electing Optional Adjustment to Basis of** [LLC] **Property**, and its regulations, address what otherwise could produce an inequity in ownership interests.

Question 12 reads:

Enter the number of Forms 8865 attached to this return ▶ _____

Another form? What is it? The answer is extremely important where a foreign LLC is involved.

The Cross Hairs of Form 8865

Form 8865 is titled: ***Return of U.S. Persons with Respect to Certain Foreign Partnerships*** [LLCs]. This is truly a formidable tax return: seven pages plus 27 pages of instructions. Among other items, the instructions define what is meant by a "U.S. Person" and the term "Certain." From our previous comments, you should be aware by now that the word "Partnership" translates directly into "Limited Liability Company" or LLC. As a result, foreign LLCs are directly in the cross hairs of Form 8865.

The term "U.S. person" means—

A citizen or resident of the U.S., a domestic LLC, a domestic corporation, and any estate or trust that is not foreign.

This is a broad swath of potential filers of the subject form. The term "resident" includes a foreign citizen residing in the U.S. under the: ***Substantial presence test*** of Section 7701(b)(3)(A) [exceeding 183 days for current and two preceding years].

The word "certain" in the title of Form 8865 refers to one of four categories of filers. A thumbnail description of each of these categories is—

Category 1 — A U.S. person owning, directly or indirectly, more than 50% interest in the foreign LLC.

Category 2 — A U.S. person owning 10% or greater interest in a foreign LLC controlled by U.S. persons each owning at least 10% interests.

Category 3 — A U.S. person contributing property to a foreign LLC in exchange for at least a 10% ownership interest therein, or whose value of property contributed exceeds $100,000.

Category 4 — A U.S. person incurring a *reportable event* with respect to a foreign LLC; such an event is either an acquisition, disposition, or change of ownership interests referenced to the "at least 10%" filing threshold.

In view of the potential ownership interests above, it is difficult to visualize a U.S. manager of a foreign LLC not having some ownership interest in the foreign entity which he manages on-site. If not directly himself, then indirectly through family members and close business associates.

Schedule K-1: 1065 vs. 8865

This may be a bit of trivia, but note the last two digits of 1065 and 8865. The two digits "65" signify a partnership return or, in our case a federal LLC return. Many income-taxing states use these same two digits to signify their partnership returns. For example, California uses Form 565 for its partnerships. The purpose for states' doing so is to better coordinate the transfer of tax information between federal and state authorities for the same class of returns being filed.

We now tell you that Schedule K-1 (1065) and Schedule K-1 (8865) have identical titles: *Partner's* [LLC Member's] *Share of Income, Credits, Deductions, etc.* Except for information differences just below the two headings, the distributive share items are identical: line-by-line, category-by-category. In fact, the instructions to Schedule K-1 (8865) say—

If more guidance is needed to complete Schedules K and K-1 of Form 8865, refer to the Form 1065 instructions.

The information portion of K-1 (8865) requires designation of the following percentages of interest in a foreign LLC:

	Start of Year	End of Year
Capital	---------------%	--------------- %
Profits	---------------%	--------------- %
Deductions	---------------%	--------------- %
Losses	---------------%	--------------- %

The 10% threshold for filing Form 8865 is that percentage which exists "at any time" during the taxable year of the foreign LLC. This 10% pertains to—

*An interest equal to 10% of the capital interest, an interest equal to 10% of the profits interest, **or** an interest to which 10% of the deductions or losses are allocated. For purposes of determining a 10% interest, the **constructive ownership** rules shall apply.*

There are two constructive ownership rules. Rule 1 pertains to entities, whereas Rule 2 pertains to individuals. Rule 1 states that—

*An interest owned **directly or indirectly by or for** a corporation, partnership [LLC], estate, or trust shall be considered as being owned proportionately by its owners.*

Rule 2 states that—

*An individual is considered to own an interest owned **directly or indirectly by or for** his family. The family of an individual incudes only that individual's spouse, brothers, sisters, ancestors, and lineal descendants.*

The constructive ownership rules are an antidote to tax-perceived evasive transactions. Such transactions are those arranged solely for the purpose of diluting ownership interests to below 10% so as to avoid any filing of Form 8865. The antidote rules are predicated upon the "economic influence" doctrine. That is, a U.S. person in an influential position may actually control 54% of a foreign LLC with only an ostensible 9% direct interest. Indirectly, he may influence five members of his close circle of family and friends, each of whom owns a 9% interest [9% + (5 x 9%) = 54%]. Tax evasive transactions are more prevalent where there are U.S. interests in foreign LLCs, foreign trusts, and foreign financial accounts. There is widespread misperception that U.S. money outside of the U.S. is "unreachable" by the IRS. Nothing could be farther from the truth.

Aliens: Resident vs. Nonresident

An alien is a foreign born person who has not acquired U.S. citizenship. For U.S. tax purposes, there are two classes of aliens: resident and nonresident. Alien individuals resident in the U.S. are taxed on their worldwide income at graduated rates, the same as U.S. citizens. Nonresident aliens are taxed the same as U.S. citizens only to the extent that their income is "effectively connected" with the active conduct of a trade or business in the U.S. Otherwise, a flat rate of 30% (or lower treaty rate) applies to "fixed or determinable" income that derives from U.S. sources which are not effectively connected with a U.S. trade or business.

The terms "resident" and "nonresident" are defined in the 2,400 statutory words of Section 7701(b): *Definition of Resident Alien and Nonresident Alien.* A resident alien is one who—

(i)   has been lawfully admitted for permanent residence in the U.S. as an immigrant in accordance with the "green card" immigration laws; or

(ii)   meets the substantial presence test of more than 183 days over a 3-year "formula period"; or

(iii) after 31 days of consecutive physical presence in the U.S. during his first year, who voluntarily elects to become a resident for tax purposes only: not for immigration purposes.

A nonresident alien is one who is neither a citizen of the U.S. nor a resident of the U.S. Residency rules are relaxed for travelers, teachers, medical care, foreign officials, etc. The tax treatment of a nonresident depends on the above-mentioned source-of-income doctrines: (a) effectively connected, and (b) fixed and determinable. That income which is not effectively connected with a trade or business within the U.S. is deemed to be "fixed or determinable," either periodically or annually. Fixed or determinable income is that which is characterized as interest, dividends, rents, royalties, pensions, annuities, salaries, wages, remuneration, and capital gains and losses on corporate stock held for investment purposes.

The term "effectively connected" income is that which derives from the active conduct of a trade or business within the U.S. The factors taken into account shall include whether—

*(A) the income, gain, or loss is derived from assets **used in** or **held for use in** the conduct of such trade or business, or*

*(B) the activities of such trade or business were **a material factor** in the realization of the income, gain, or loss* [IRC Sec. 864(c)(2)].

A foreign LLC doing business in the U.S. via a U.S. resident manager is clearly an effectively connected trade or business. Thus, also, is the distributive share of income, gain, or loss that passes through to the nonresident member-owners of the LLC entity.

Withholding at Source

Nonresident aliens and foreign corporations who are members of a U.S. managed foreign LLC are subject to draconian withholding-at-source rules. We say "draconian" because the withholdings are at the highest tax rates permissible under U.S. law; the rates are applied to the highest possible effectively connected taxable income; and the withholdings are treated as "deemed distributions of basis" until U.S. nonresident income tax returns are filed by an LLC member. Whenever an ownership interest is sold or otherwise transferred, after there has been a deemed distribution of basis, maximum capital gains result . . . and maximum withholdings occur. The preemptive mandate for these rules is IRC Section 1446.

Section 1446 is titled: ***Withholding Tax on Amounts Paid by Partnerships to Foreign Partners***. As always with federal LLC matters, the word "partnerships" has to be read as "LLC entities" and the word "partners" as "LLC members." The thrust of Section 1446 is that a foreign LLC conducting business in the U.S. is treated as a corporation for tax computation and withholding purposes. This means that an entity-level tax is imposed, withheld, and paid over (to the U.S. Treasury) before there is any pass-through of distributive share items to individual members. For an understanding of the concept we are describing, we present Figure 12.3. The withholding applies also to the gross proceeds derived from the disposition of real property in the U.S., by its foreign owners [Section 1445].

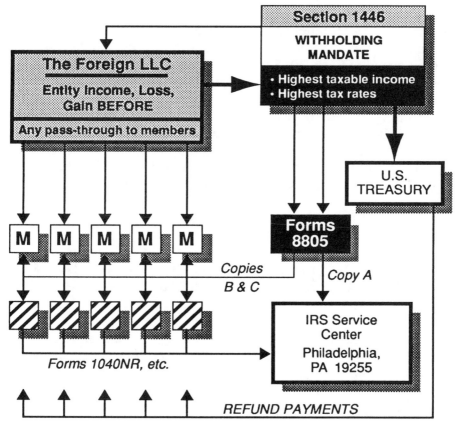

Fig. 12.3 - The Intentional Tax Over-Withholding on Foreign LLC Members

The withholding and payover require special tax forms of their own. This should come as no surprise. There are three such forms, namely:

Form 8804 — *Annual Return for Partnership Withholding Tax (Section 1446)*

Form 8805 — *Foreign Partner's Information Statement of Section 1446 Withholding Tax*

Form 8813 — *Partnership Withholding Tax Payment Voucher (Section 1446)*

These forms are prepared by the Withholding Agent: the U.S. manager of the foreign LLC. When completed, the forms are sent separately to the IRS Service Center in Philadelphia, PA. They are **not** attached to Form 1065 (the "Return of Income") for the LLC.

It is Form 8805 that is significant for each LLC foreign member. It indicates not only the type of member: individual, corporation, other; it also shows in abbreviated manner how the withholding tax was computed. Because of the off-the-top way of computing the maximum-possible taxable income at the LLC entity level, the withholding amount is guaranteed to exceed that which would actually be due, when and if a nonresident return is filed.

Nonresident Returns: Form 1040NR

Two copies of Form 8805 (Withholding Statement) are transmitted to each foreign withholdee. **Copy B** is marked: *Keep for your records*; **Copy C** is marked: *Attach to your Federal tax return*. The very last line on both of these copies says—

Total tax credit allowed to partner [LLC member] *under Section 1446. Claim this amount as a credit against your U.S. income tax on Form 1040NR ... etc.*   ▶ _____

The clear implication is that, if a foreign resident (with effectively connected income from a trade or business within the U.S.) does not file a U.S. tax return, the U.S. Treasury keeps his withheld money. It does so knowing full well that the withheld amount far exceeds the true tax amount. The burden of proof is on the withholdee to come forward and stake his claim for a refund.

Form 1040NR is titled: *U.S. Nonresident Alien Income Tax Return*. The 1040NR applies not only to foreign individuals, it applies also to foreign estates and trusts (who are LLC members).

Among the usual items in the headportion of a tax return, the filer is asked:

Of what country were you a citizen or national during the tax year? ▶ _____
*Give address **outside of the U.S.** to which you want any refund check mailed.*

Excluding attachments, Form 1040NR is a 5-page form . . . plus 32 pages of instructions. Pages 1 and 2 are similar in format to the corresponding pages of Form 1040 for citizens and residents of the U.S. Beyond this format similarity, the 1040NR is far more complicated than a 1040. Three reasons account for this added complexity:

[A]   The income items on page 1 are only those amounts which are "effectively connected" with a U.S. trade or business. This requires a careful reading of the instructions so as to avoid any non-U.S. sources of income.

[B]   The income and tax on U.S. sources **not** effectively connected with a U.S. trade or business are itemized separately on page 4. This itemization includes any capital gains or losses from the sale or exchange of property in the U.S.

[C]   Page 5: *Other Information*, tries to nail down the filer's citizenship, his passport number, and when entry to, or departure from, the U.S. were made (if any); whether the filer is a dual-status taxpayer; whether the filer is an expatriate; and the filer's total foreign source income not effectively connected with a U.S. trade or business.

A conscientious foreign resident could easily get the impression that Form 1040NR is deliberately designed to discourage its filing. This could be. But there's a dollarized carrot in the *Payments* portion of the form on its page 2. A preprinted line there reads—

U.S. tax withheld at source:

- From other than "effectively connected" sources $_____
- By partnerships [LLCs] under Section 1446 $_____
- On disposition of U.S. real property interests $_____

If there is an excess of these withholdings over the tax computed, the filer is given the choice of receiving a U.S. refund check at his foreign address or authorizing its direct deposit electronically into his U.S. bank account (if he has one).

X X X X X

In closing this chapter and this book, we make a philosophical observation. From the point of view of free trade and globalization of the world, the filing of U.S. nonresident income tax returns conveys a superb subliminal message. Such returns, we think, influence the greater use of the U.S. dollar as an international currency, and the greater use of English as an international language. No other tax system in the world is as intrusive into the financial affairs of individuals — whether domestic or foreign — as is the Internal Revenue Code.

ABOUT

THE AUTHOR

Holmes F. Crouch

Born on a small farm in southern Maryland, Holmes was graduated from the U.S. Coast Guard Academy with a Bachelor's Degree in Marine Engineering. While serving on active duty, he wrote many technical articles on maritime matters. After attaining the rank of Lieutenant Commander, he resigned to pursue a career as a nuclear engineer.

Continuing his education, he earned a Master's Degree in Nuclear Engineering from the University of California. He also authored two books on nuclear propulsion. As a result of the tax write-offs associated with writing these books, the IRS audited his returns. The IRS's handling of the audit procedure so annoyed Holmes that he undertook to become as knowledgeable as possible regarding tax procedures. He became a licensed private Tax Practitioner by passing an examination administered by the IRS. Having attained this credential, he started his own tax preparation and counseling business in 1972.

In the early years of his tax practice, he was a regular talk-show guest on San Francisco's KGO Radio responding to hundreds of phone-in tax questions from listeners. He was a much sought-after guest speaker at many business seminars and taxpayer meetings. He also provided counseling on special tax problems, such as divorce matters, property exchanges, timber harvesting, mining ventures, animal breeding, independent contractors, selling businesses, and offices-at-home. Over the past 25 years, he has prepared well over 10,000 tax returns for individuals, estates, trusts, and small businesses (in partnership and corporate form).

During the tax season of January through April, he prepares returns in a unique manner. During a single meeting, he completes the return . . . *on the spot!* The client leaves with his return signed, sealed, and in a stamped envelope. His unique approach to preparing returns and his personal interest in his clients' tax affairs have honed his professional proficiency. His expertise extends through itemized deductions, computer-matching of income sources, capital gains and losses, business expenses and cost of goods, residential rental expenses, limited and general partnership activities, closely-held corporations, to family farms and ranches.

He remembers spending 12 straight hours completing a doctor's complex return. The next year, the doctor, having moved away, utilized a large accounting firm to prepare his return. Their accountant was so impressed by the manner in which the prior return was prepared that he recommended the doctor travel the 500 miles each year to have Holmes continue doing it.

He recalls preparing a return for an unemployed welder, for which he charged no fee. Two years later the welder came back and had his return prepared. He paid the regular fee . . . and then added a $300 tip.

During the off season, he represents clients at IRS audits and appeals. In one case a shoe salesman's audit was scheduled to last three hours. However, after examining Holmes' documentation it was concluded in 15 minutes with "no change" to his return. In another instance he went to an audit of a custom jeweler that the IRS dragged out for more than six hours. But, supported by Holmes' documentation, the client's return was accepted by the IRS with "no change."

Then there was the audit of a language translator that lasted two full days. The auditor scrutinized more than $1.25 million in gross receipts, all direct costs, and operating expenses. Even though all expensed items were documented and verified, the auditor decided that more than $23,000 of expenses ought to be listed as capital items for depreciation instead. If this had been enforced it would have resulted in a significant additional amount of tax. Holmes strongly disagreed and after many hours of explanation got the amount reduced by more than 60% on behalf of his client.

He has dealt extensively with gift, death and trust tax returns. These preparations have involved him in the tax aspects of wills, estate planning, trustee duties, probate, marital and charitable bequests, gift and death exemptions, and property titling.

Although not an attorney, he prepares Petitions to the U.S. Tax Court for clients. He details the IRS errors and taxpayer facts by citing pertinent sections of tax law and regulations. In a recent case involving an attorney's ex-spouse, the IRS asserted a tax deficiency of $155,000. On behalf of his client, he petitioned the Tax Court and within six months the IRS conceded the case.

Over the years, Holmes has observed that the IRS is not the industrious, impartial, and competent federal agency that its official public imaging would have us believe.

He found that, at times, under the slightest pretext, the IRS has interpreted against a taxpayer in order to assess maximum penalties, and may even delay pending matters so as to increase interest due on additional taxes. He has confronted the IRS in his own behalf on five separate occasions, going before the U.S. Claims Court, U.S. District Court, and U.S. Tax Court. These were court actions that tested specific sections of the Internal Revenue Code which he found ambiguous, inequitable, and abusively interpreted by the IRS.

Disturbed by the conduct of the IRS and by the general lack of tax knowledge by most individuals, he began an innovative series of taxpayer-oriented Federal tax guides. To fulfill this need, he undertook the writing of a series of guidebooks that provide in-depth knowledge on one tax subject at a time. He focuses on subjects that plague taxpayers all throughout the year. Hence, his formulation of the "Allyear" Tax Guide series.

The author is indebted to his wife, Irma Jean, and daughter, Barbara MacRae, for the word processing and computer graphics that turn his experiences into the reality of these publications. Holmes welcomes comments, questions, and suggestions from his readers. He can be contacted in California at (408) 867-2628, or by writing to the publisher's address.

ALLYEAR Tax Guides
by Holmes F. Crouch

For information about the above titles,
and/or a free 8 page catalog, contact:

www.allyeartax.com

Phone: (408) 867-2628   Fax: (408) 867-6466